the
MODERN
HIPPIE
table

the
MODERN
HIPPIE
Table

Recipes and Menus for
Eating Simply and Living Beautifully

———————————

LAUREN THOMAS

Photographs by Kristy Horst

XO,
Lauren

THE
collective
BOOK STUDIO

Library of Congress Cataloging-in-
Publication Data available.

ISBN: 978-1-68555-006-6
Ebook ISBN: 978-1-68555-007-3
LCCN: 2021924392

Manufactured in China.
Photographs by Kristy Horst.
Food Styling by Frankie Chacon.
Cover and Interior Design by
Chris Enter and AJ Hansen.

10 9 8 7 6 5 4 3 2 1

The Collective Book Studio®
Oakland, California
www.thecollectivebook.studio

FOR ALL WHO DOUBT THEMSELVES IN THE PURSUIT
OF CHASING DREAMS,
DO NOT FEAR YOUR OWN LIGHT;
YOU ARE THE AUTHOR OF YOUR DESTINY.

CONTENTS

DESSERTS

DRINKS

A GUIDE TO DRINKING WHISKEY

Introduction

—

The best recipes aren't just homemade, they're homegrown. And by homegrown, I mean that the best conversations and life lessons happen around a table laden with everyone's favorite foods. Family bonds and lifetime friendships can be cultivated every day by creating simple, intentional spaces for gathering. In fact, your dining room table is a blank canvas just waiting for this to happen. When friends and families are brought together through good food and meaningful conversation, it's a chance to be seen and heard—to be present. This way of slowing down, showing up, and restoring a simpler life in a fast-paced world is the genesis of what I call "Modern Hippie." For me, Modern Hippie describes a place where old meets new, simple meets sophisticated, and fancy meets fun. It's an inviting atmosphere with whimsically elegant tables showcasing uncomplicated traditional foods enhanced with fresh twists. In the kitchen and at the table, Modern Hippie is the love language I share to inspire everyone to find joy in the lost art of cooking and entertaining in a fun, approachable way.

In my family when I was growing up, food and tradition were woven together, and my mother's and grandmothers' cooking were like a religion to me. I can easily remember the intoxicating aromas, comforting rituals, and feelings of togetherness they inspired within our home. It is my hope and intention to encourage you to curate the same kind of welcoming sustenance and surroundings that will give rise to good times like the ones I was so fortunate to experience, and to create your own memories and relationships that will last well beyond the actual experience.

In the *Modern Hippie Table*, I share some of my family's favorite dishes along with the recipes I created myself. Each one is simple enough to prepare easily so you can spend less time in the kitchen and more time with your loved ones. Some of the recipes are made from scratch and others make creative use of store-bought convenience foods and premade products that will save you time. It is part of my Modern Hippie philosophy to buy quality ingredients that are organic whenever possible, and I substitute healthier alternatives for gluten and dairy more often than not. There are plenty of appetizers and snacks, salads, and main dishes, plus some indulgent desserts and drinks to round things out. You won't want to miss my husband Christian's Classic Italian Pasta (page 116) or my Cilantro Lime Rock Shrimp Tacos (page 100), which have become favorites of both my family and friends. And I particularly love the section on charcuterie boards (pages 163–77), which are great for larger parties as well as smaller, more intimate gatherings.

While I pride myself on the discipline of cooking, the scope of Modern Hippie goes well beyond the food. It's a passion of mine to make sure the surroundings are as beautiful as the meal is delicious, so I've included ideas to design simple tablescapes using flowers and linens that complement whatever I'm serving. My emphasis is always to decorate in a straightforward way that doesn't add stress or break the bank. Finally, suggested menus are sprinkled throughout the book to help you plan out themed meals, and with each menu, I've shared tips on how to set the scene for the occasion. This way, you'll have the confidence to get your creative plans started and the time-saving tips to pull it off.

Whether I'm cooking, entertaining, or traveling, creating experiences with this kind of laid-back elegance is a lifestyle that is doable for everyone and it's one I love sharing.

Celebrating life, every day, is the Modern Hippie way.

XO,

Lauren

SETTING
THE SCENE

Creating Intentional Spaces

———

I put as much thought into setting the scene for entertaining as I do wrapping a gift. What people see and how they feel when they first walk in the door sets the tone for the occasion, and it can be equally as important as the food you serve. My husband is an architect, and from watching him design, I've learned the importance of creating inviting spaces for people to occupy. When guests walk into the energy of our home, I feel a sense of responsibility to make them feel like a part of our family.

Cooking is a passion for me, but creating an atmosphere where people feel special, important, and comfortable is what really matters to me and what I love the most. I think a good host lets people know what to expect before the evening begins, and it creates a vibe that makes people feel pampered from the moment they walk in the door. Everything should be thought out and intentionally executed, such as having a place set aside for coats and purses, offering drinks and something to snack on right away, providing somewhere comfortable to sit, and facilitating good conversation. Whether the mood for your evening is informal and loungy or sophisticated and fancy, a host's goal is universally simple: create an experience where people enjoy themselves so much that they will remember the positive way they felt when they were your guests. Imagine the gift you can give to your family and friends by creating a space that allows for this to happen in your home. No number of guests is too small or too large and no occasion is too insignificant to celebrate the true essence of life, which is all around us, every day. Paying attention to this is not only part of experiencing true joy, but it's also spreading it to others.

A Love Affair with Hosting

My grandparents were big entertainers. Grammy planned all her evenings carefully, no matter the occasion. Sometimes she'd sit down with a stationer months before a big event and come up with clever phrases to put on the invitations for her guests. Occasions of any size were celebrated, from our graduations and engagements to small birthday parties and Sunday night family dinners. I remember paying attention to every detail as she focused on what would make guests feel most welcome in their home, such as greeting each one at the door, escorting them to the bar where drinks and hors d'oeuvres were offered, and having the piano on self-play mode. I even remember how she would tell jokes as conversation icebreakers. There was always laughter and I was aware of how much everyone, including me, felt welcomed, happy, and comfortable. Amid all the hustle and bustle that went into the bigger gatherings, there was always a brief sense of calm just before guests arrived-—and I loved the excitement of anticipation and that feeling of knowing that everything was ready. The music playing, the lighting on point, the enticing aromas of the soon-to-be-served meal in the air, and the way I felt in my dress; I suppose that is where my love affair with hosting began.

To this day, I take all the senses into consideration when I host an evening, not only those of my guests but my own as well. It's important for me to enjoy hosting and for my guests and family to feel that positive energy from me. My favorite way to host is by holding small, casual gatherings where I'll wear a flowy dress and kick off my shoes, but no matter what kind of event you are planning, the one common theme to remember as a host is to plan intentionally so that you and your guests always feel "at home."

Planning Ahead

—

When it comes to planning an evening, I always start with the menu. A meal such as a barbecue or taco night calls for a more casual theme and atmosphere, whereas a New Year's Eve party or a bridal shower luncheon has a more elegant feel. Either way, the food you serve should highlight the atmosphere you're trying to accomplish with the occasion. Then, you can figure out how to plan your evening so that you can maximize the time you spend with your guests. For example, if you want to serve a heartier meal that is more time-consuming to cook, consider making it ahead and heating it up just before serving. A common mistake people make when having company over for dinner is cooking a meal that requires too much attention in the kitchen and the host ends up missing out on being with their guests. Reflecting on my earlier days of hosting, I regret some of my decisions because I was cooking and cleaning while my guests were drinking cocktails, and it was distracting, for them and for me.

To avoid that, I now plan so that the bulk of the meal is prepared earlier in the evening before guests arrive, and when they are actually there, I can enjoy their company without worrying about the meal. For example, if I know I want to showcase the main meal that I'm making from scratch, I'll spend most of the earlier part of the day preparing the appetizers and desserts ahead of time so that they are ready to serve without taking my attention away from my guests. This way, I can focus on the parts of my main meal that require my attention and take the least amount of effort. Prior to their arrival, I will also have the table set, the bar will be set up with ice, and sliced citrus or pre-batched cocktails will be ready in a pitcher. I'll set some glassware out on the bar depending on which drinks we'll be serving. A charcuterie board will be on the table in the room where we will be having cocktails and talking prior to sitting down for dinner. Music will be playing and the playlist or records will be selected in advance. The idea here is to enjoy as much precious time with your guests as possible, and planning ahead affords you that.

It can be tempting to make "fancy" food to impress your guests, but I can assure you that fancy does not necessarily mean better. People coming to your home will be drawn to more casual comfort food—foods that are not complicated or time-consuming to prepare— because they came to see you. If you're less stressed, your guests will enjoy themselves more. I love serving simple, delicious foods that feed the soul and lend to the memorability of the evening. I've had friends mention over a year later that they can't wait to have my Rosemary Onion Mac and Cheese (page 161) again because they remember how happy they were when they ate it. This is a dish that takes a little more time and effort, but it can be made ahead and it's often the focal point of the evening, especially when the theme for the evening is "Southern cuisine." Likewise, if you're planning a bar-becue, which often requires time and labor away from your guests, and you plan to make Tender, Crispy Barbecue Ribs (page 133), cook the ribs in the oven ahead of time and preheat the grill just before guests arrive.

In that recipe and many others in the book, I share time-saving tips that ensure that everyone is satisfied and happy. Use the menus throughout the book as inspiration to plan your meals. I've organized the menus into themes or occasions for you to reference, and I've suggested how to set the scene for each one. Use them as a jump-ing-off point for creating your own unique gatherings.

When I plan out the menu, I like to keep things a little more casual and simple, so I don't get custom-printed invitations like Grammy used to do. But I do like to make things more fun by using a design application I found for my phone where I can create a similar kind of invitation quickly and easily. I usually include the themed menu for the evening on the invite and I text or email it to guests a day or two ahead of time. For example, if I'm having friends over at the begin-ning of summer, I'll choose a fun, simple background that leaves plenty of space to write, such as a blue sky with a palm tree off to the side. I'll use a fun font style and call the event a "Summer Kickoff Barbecue." This is a special touch that will help increase anticipation for the event and it has the added bonus of giving your guests an idea of what to bring. (In my experience, even if you say, "Just bring your-selves!" people tend to bring something anyway.) If I can help them by giving them the theme in advance so they can bring something that contributes to the enjoyment of the evening, I'm all for it.

Planning Your Spaces to Entertain

—

My ideal version of entertaining at home involves no more than four to six guests, but regardless of the size of the gathering, my husband and I plan out the spaces in and around the house where we will start and end the night. Typically, we begin the night by bringing guests into our kitchen, serving them appetizers and shaking up some cocktails to engage all their senses and give them a glimpse of what's cooking. Then, we usually move cocktails and appetizers into the sitting room, where we can partake in more engaging conversation. At this point, the bulk of my meal has been made and the guests have my full attention. Depending on the temperamental South Florida weather, we might enjoy the main course outdoors on our long wooden table or keep the evening inside in the dining room. I'll make sure the table is set, the water poured, and the candles lit before inviting everyone to sit down. When the meal is finished, I serve dessert at the main table or invite everyone to move back into the sitting room for after-dinner drinks.

Tablescaping

—

Just like landscaping makes your yard look beautiful and intentionally put together, tablescaping does that for your table. I love transporting guests from their everyday surroundings to a more intimate atmosphere at my table by creating a cozy, inviting dining experience. This seems to be a lost art these days, not just because people are so busy but also because they're often intimidated and don't know where to start. I'm here to tell you that you've got this! Creating a memorable setting is not hard and it doesn't need to be time-consuming. You'll see the words "simple" and "elegant" quite a bit throughout this book because that's a look that is both beautiful *and* doable for most people. One thing to keep in mind is that the menus and recipes in this book are specifically designed to give you a little extra time to make the table look nice. And most people already have the items they'll need to decorate in and around their home. For example, a simple water pitcher can double as a glass vase for flowers, and small votive candle holders make great bud vases. Also, if you are hosting more people than you have matching cloth napkins, no worries! You can always mix and match similar or complementary color palettes such as beige and ivory.

Just like with the menu, an elegant tablescape is all about thoughtful planning and the creative and intentional use of what's available to you. For a simple, elegant tablescape for any occasion, try one or more of the tips on the following pages.

TABLECLOTHS, RUNNERS, AND BARE TABLES

Depending on the atmosphere you want to express for the event, decide whether you'd like to use a fabric runner or tablecloth, which is more traditional, or go for something more casual and natural, such as overlapping palm leaves or a combination of moss and flowers to accent the middle of the table. The materials and colors you choose will set the tone for the rest of the table. For example, I've used a thin white bedsheet for my outdoor table covering, which can be whimsically beautiful. (I find that it can be frustrating to find tablecloths that fit properly, and they can be cumbersome to store, so I buy sheets just for this purpose.) I like to use neutral colors for the first layer on the table. They create a base on which I can mix and match a monochromatic color scheme with place mats and napkins, and then I brighten up the table with florals. Alternatively, if you have a table made from natural wood, you may opt to leave it uncovered for a more boho-chic rustic look. Table runners are a great way to add dimension to the table yet still allow the table to peek through.

PLACE MATS, CHARGERS, AND NAPKINS

Once you have a first layer on the table, playing around with place mats, chargers, and napkins can be fun. They will frame the plate and you can layer them to create whatever look you want. I love using natural elements for tablescapes, such as flat palm leaves, and I'll place them under my plates as a nice natural frame for each table setting. I have a collection of fabric napkins in several color palettes, which I can mix and match if I need to accommodate more people. Accenting with napkin rings is fun, but it's not necessary to have them. You can tie up napkins with natural jute twine to enhance an earthy, romantic "Modern Hippie" feel. One of my favorite things to do with napkins is to slide the stems of flowers, greenery, or fresh herbs into the rings or twine.

TABLEWARE

Keep it minimal. I keep two full sets of dishware, glassware, and silverware in my kitchen—enough to serve ten people. One set of dishes is modern and white, and the other is more rustic and ivory. You can't go wrong with this neutral color palette, and you can always combine neutral-colored sets if you're having more people. Frankly, if I had more room in my kitchen, I'd keep an extra set of slate-gray plates to create a different, moodier look. I like to combine monochromatic plate colors by layering a salad plate on top of a dinner plate instead of placing a salad bowl off to the side of each plate. Building layers of color can look really beautiful as long as it's thought out and done intentionally. I like to collect mismatched glasses that I've purchased at home-discount stores or at after-holiday sales. For water glassware, I keep one set each of short and tall tumblers on hand, as well as shabby-chic etched vintage tumblers for a romantic, elegant look, or stemless wineglasses for a more modern option. Glassware can be mixed and matched just like your cloth napkins, as long as you keep one element the same, such as size, color palette, or texture. For utensils, I keep one set of modern silverware and one set of brass flatware on hand. These can be mixed and matched too.

FLORALS AND GREENERY

I believe that no tablescape is complete without incorporating florals and greenery, or some element of nature. I design most of my tablescapes around things I already have in and around my home, and my design for the table typically starts with the natural foliage that I have access to. We live in the tropical climate of South Florida, so oftentimes I'll use seasonal foliage from my yard or around my neighborhood as table decor. Whether entertaining indoors or outdoors, I'll use a beautiful palm frond or a cluster of sea grapes instead of a charger under a plate. If you don't have access to greenery and florals around your yard or neighborhood due to location or climate, you could use sticks and twigs placed minimally and strategically in the center of the table peeking out from serving platters or vases. Acorns, pine cones, succulents, and moss can all make beautiful accents for a natural tablescape. No matter what the color or season you find yourself in, nature is always the most beautiful and affordable material to use for tablescapes.

For centerpieces, try mixing store-bought roses with the beautiful flowery outer leaves of cabbage or kale, or some other form of edible greenery, as green filler. The leaves of cabbage have been removed by the time they get to your grocery store shelf, but you can find them at farmers' markets, or if you are lucky, you could grow them in your own garden! Use one centerpiece for a small round table, or use three for a larger rectangular table. Odd numbers are magic numbers! The most important thing to remember is to keep the arrangements low so that guests can see each other across the table and they can easily pass dishes, if necessary.

I consider roses to be a symbol of beauty, innocence, and love, so they usually adorn my tables (as well as the bedrooms and bathrooms around my house). Small bud vases with a cluster of roses or sprigs of fresh herbs make lovely mini arrangements to put in front of each plate, especially if you have leftover herbs and greens from the meal you're creating. Imagine how special your guests will feel when

they have their own personal bouquet of flowers. Mini bud vases are inexpensive and make a great parting gift for your company to bring home as an evening memento.

For a romantic table—my favorite look for any occasion—I buy two bunches of flowers from my local market or grocery store and arrange one bunch in a short vase in the center of my dining table. With the other bunch, I combine one or two buds with some greenery and stick them into small bud vases scattered around the table, which adds dimension. For the finishing touch, I nestle mini tea lights and some moss into an assortment of votive candle holders or small mason jars, and place them between the main arrangements.

SEATING

Whether you use tags or place cards to tell guests where to sit is up to you. I like to do this even for smaller gatherings of four or six guests because it makes everyone feel a little more special. I keep some neutral-colored textured paper around and I cut them into small rectangles and spell out names in script. For example, I like to tie the place cards onto napkin rings with natural jute twine, or around the mini bud vases in front of each plate. Additionally, you can get creative with the natural elements I mentioned in the previous section by using a gold permanent marker to write names in script on sea grapes, palm fronds, fall leaves, or even small rocks.

Setting the Mood and Groove

—

We are a musical family. My husband loves to play the guitar and we all enjoy picking out records to play on our turntable. On nights when both of my teenagers are home, sitting around listening to music while enjoying good conversation is something we really love to do. It's an activity that brings us closer together by making time for each other. Listening to music allows people to slow down, stimulates conversation, and invites another dimension of creative expression into households where families are often so busy with conflicting work and activity schedules. The same holds true for the dinner table and for hosting gatherings. I like to assign music playlist selections to my kids when we have family dinners because it's a way of letting them choose an element of the atmosphere and feel included, and it's not just me putting dinner on the table. Dining together is more than just eating food; it's a way of participating in an intentional activity. When everyone participates on some level by contributing to the tone of the evening, it's a great way to show up for one another.

When choosing music for guests, think about the mood you're trying to convey. Whether softly playing in the background or meant to encourage people to dance, the music will set the tone for the evening. A good rule of thumb is that the music should be loud enough for guests to hear but soft enough so people don't feel the

need to shout over it. Fortunately, with modern technology, we don't have to interrupt conversation to change records. At our house, we choose a playlist ahead of time that will play continuously throughout the night. If it's a hot summer night and I'm entertaining outside, we might play Latin or Cuban music. If we're eating inside, we usually go for soft jazz, and some of my favorites are from Etta James and Miles Davis. I also love to play Norah Jones or Stan Getz when I'm cooking and I'll pour myself a glass of wine to sip on while I work. No matter what sort of tunes you enjoy, there is almost always a place for music when entertaining.

Just as music sets the tone, the lighting you choose will also contribute to the mood and feel of the evening. My husband is very particular about this element. "It's the most important thing," he says, "because it's the first thing that is sensed when a person walks into a room and it conveys a level of intimacy. It adds intrigue and builds mystery." Everyone has been in a room or been stuck sitting under a lamp that's too bright. Bright lights are for football games and hospitals, not for intimate gatherings. Create a warm and inviting ambience by dimming overhead lights in all of your entertaining spaces and by using candles in your cocktail area and on the dining room table. Unscented candlesticks and votives are a must for the dinner table because you don't want the fragrance from the candles to compete with the deliciousness of the food. For outdoor tables and spaces, bistro lights are most effective because they are dim enough to cast a romantic and inviting glow overhead, but bright enough so you can see the food in front of you and the faces across from you.

Now that you have the tools to set the scene for a beautiful table and atmosphere, let's explore some delicious modern comfort food for you and your guests to enjoy.

BREAKFAST

YOGURT PARFAIT CUPS

—

This is a flavorful and colorful breakfast choice and makes a beautiful presentation when served in stemless wineglasses. For special occasions such as brunches and showers, double or triple the recipe and serve these on a tray or in a crate with a variety of extra toppings in small mason jars on the side. These can be made ahead of time and stored in the fridge. I like using Greek yogurt for my base because it's thick and creamy, but use whatever yogurt you like, including dairy-free. Choose your favorite granola or crumble up my famous Protein-Packed Granola Bars (page 61). Serves 4.

- 4 cups vanilla Greek yogurt

- 4 cups granola

- 4 cups mixed berries, such as blueberries, blackberries, and sliced strawberries

- Honey, for drizzling

Place ¼ cup of yogurt in the bottom of four drinking glasses, followed by ¼ cup of granola and ¼ cup of mixed berries, making sure that each layer is spread out to the edges of the glass. Repeat each layer one more time, with the last layer being mixed berries. Drizzle honey over the top. Serve cold.

 Tip: When serving a crowd, get creative with the toppings and place them in small containers so your guests can customize their own parfaits. Chia seeds, bee pollen, toasted coconut, sliced almonds, and pistachios are some of my toppings of choice.

SKILLET FRITTATA FROM LEFTOVERS

—

When we took family summer trips to the Bahamas, my Uncle Rick made frittatas for brunch using veggies or meats left over from dinner the night before, and they were delicious. Frittatas are great for serving to a crowd, whether it's a holiday breakfast or a brunch-themed shower, because you can serve them hot or at room temperature. They also store well in the fridge and you can pack them up for work or school lunches. Here I use onions, spinach, mushrooms, sausage, and Swiss cheese, but you can throw in almost anything you find in your fridge. Serves 6 to 8.

- 12 eggs

- 3 tablespoons whole or low-fat milk

- 1 cup shredded Swiss cheese

- 1 teaspoon black pepper

- ½ teaspoon salt

- 2 tablespoons coconut oil

- 1 large white onion, chopped

- 1 cup chopped mushrooms

- 2 cups packed spinach

- 1 cup chopped cooked sausage

Preheat the oven to 425°F.

In a large bowl, whisk together the eggs, milk, cheese, pepper, and salt until well blended. Set aside.

Continued

Heat the oil in a 12-inch cast-iron skillet over medium heat until it shimmers, about 3 minutes. Add the onion and mushrooms and cook, stirring occasionally, until fragrant, about 3 minutes. Add the spinach and cooked sausage and cook, stirring, until mixed well with the other vegetables and the spinach wilts, about 1 minute.

Whisk the egg mixture once more and pour the mixture into the skillet with the vegetables and sausage. Using a large spoon, stir briefly to combine the ingredients. Cook until the outside edge of the frittata turns lighter in color, about 2 minutes.

Carefully transfer the skillet to the oven and bake for 10 to 12 minutes, or until the eggs are puffed and the center of the eggs barely move when you give the skillet a light shake. Carefully remove the pan from the oven and place on a cooling rack for 5 minutes before cutting into slices. Serve warm.

Weekend Brunch Menu

MIMOSAS

SKILLET FRITTATA FROM LEFTOVERS (page 29)

TOASTED BUNS WITH JAM (page 40)

CINNAMON BUN TWISTS (page 166)

FRESH BERRIES

—

SET THE SCENE

The night before, set up the buffet serving pieces, plates, flatware, and napkins.

Cut and prep the veggies for the frittata and bake the Cinnamon Bun Twists. Buy fresh berries such as blueberries, blackberries, and/or strawberries, place them in a serving bowl, and refrigerate.

Create a playlist of soft jazz or queue up a list from the Internet so you're ready to press play in the morning.

Buy two bunches of flowers from your local market or grocery store and arrange one in a short vase in the center of your table. With the other bunch, snip buds or greenery and stick one or two into small bud vases scattered around the table where you'll be eating.

MY GRANDMOTHER'S EGGS BENEDICT

—

To me, there is nothing that smells more like home than the aroma of eggs Benedict cooking in my grandmother's kitchen. My brother and I used to spend Saturday nights at her house and we'd wake up to our choice of eggs Benedict, pancakes, bacon, sausage—whatever we wanted. She always used a packaged hollandaise sauce, such as Knorr, which tastes delicious and I've come to realize it's a real time-saver. Adding brandy gives it a nice extra kick! Serves 4.

- 2 (0.9-ounce) packages hollandaise sauce mix

- 2 cups low-fat milk

- ½ cup butter

- 2 tablespoons brandy (optional)

- 4 English muffins, halved

- 16 slices Canadian bacon

- 2 tablespoons white vinegar

- 8 eggs

- Salt and black pepper

- Chopped fresh chives

- Paprika

Preheat the oven to a low broil. Place a rack in the top third of the oven.

In a small saucepan over medium-high heat, combine the dry hollandaise mix with the milk and butter and prepare according to the package instructions. Add the brandy, if using, and whisk until combined. Turn the heat to low and keep warm, stirring occasionally, until you are ready to serve.

Continued

On a large baking sheet, arrange the English muffins in a single layer with the cut-side up. Broil until the muffins are toasted and light brown, about 3 minutes. Flip the muffins over, and broil for 1 minute. Transfer the baking sheet to a cooling rack and set aside.

On a smaller baking sheet, arrange the Canadian bacon in a single layer. Broil until the bacon has steam coming off the top, about 2 minutes. Flip over the bacon and broil for another 2 minutes. Transfer the pan to a cooling rack and set aside.

Fill a 6-quart saucepan with several inches of water and add the vinegar. Bring the water to a boil over high heat. Turn the heat down and keep the water at a low boil with only a few bubbles coming up every now and then. Working quickly, crack one egg at a time into a small bowl or ramekin and carefully slip the egg into the water. Cook until the eggs float to the top, about 3 minutes. Using a slotted spoon, transfer the eggs to a plate.

Top each English muffin half with two slices of Canadian bacon and one poached egg. Spoon the desired amount of sauce over each egg muffin. Season with salt and black pepper to taste. Serve immediately.

AVOCADO TOAST TWO WAYS

—

I absolutely love the avocado toast craze, but avocados weren't my favorite growing up. As I've discovered with many foods, I developed a palate for them as an adult. And it's a good thing, because they're a tasty and healthy alternative to cream cheese. When it comes to bread, there is no better crunch, in my opinion, than toasted sourdough bread, which is why I always keep thick precut slices in the freezer. Here are two versions of avocado toast that are favorites in our home. They both call for sprouts or microgreens, but if these are not available to you, arugula is a nice flavorful substitute. Each variety serves 1.

Smoked Salmon and Capers

- 2 (1-inch) slices sourdough bread, toasted

- 1 medium ripe avocado, pitted and peeled

- 1 teaspoon everything bagel seasoning

- 2 Campari or Roma tomatoes, thinly sliced

- 4 ounces Alaskan smoked salmon (preferably wild-caught)

- 1 tablespoon capers

- 1 tablespoon crumbled feta cheese

- 1 small handful sunflower sprouts or other microgreens

Top each slice of toast with half the avocado, ½ teaspoon of everything bagel seasoning, 2 or 3 slices of tomato, half the smoked salmon, ½ tablespoon of capers, 1 tablespoon of feta, and half the microgreens equally. Serve immediately.

Continued

Tomato, Radish, and Feta

- 2 (1-inch) slices sourdough bread, toasted

- 1 medium ripe avocado, pitted and peeled

- Salt

- 2 Campari or Roma tomatoes, thinly sliced

- 1 medium radish, thinly sliced

- 1 tablespoon crumbled feta cheese

- Balsamic glaze, for drizzling

- 1 small handful microgreens

On each slice of toast, spread half the avocado evenly and sprinkle with salt to taste. Top each slice of toast with 3 slices of tomato, 3 slices of radish, and ½ tablespoon of feta. Drizzle with the balsamic glaze and divide the microgreens equally over the top. Serve immediately.

OPEN-FACED EGG SANDWICH WITH GUAVA JAM

—

Guava jam was introduced to me by my grandfather, and to this day, the taste of it still reminds me of him. When I was young, he would make me buttered toast with guava jam with a sunny-side-up egg on the side. This recipe is a twist on my childhood favorite, and I made it a little more special by leaving off the top slice of bread and serving it with a fork and knife. You won't want to use just any bread for this. I buy sourdough bread from a local bakery, slice it thick, and store it in the freezer so I'll always have sliced bread ready for egg sandwiches or avocado toast. Serve it with a side of fresh fruit for a completely satisfying breakfast. Serves 2.

- 2 thick slices sourdough bread

- ½ tablespoon butter

- 4 tablespoons guava jam

- 1 tablespoon coconut oil

- 4 eggs

- Smoked paprika, for sprinkling

- Salt and black pepper

- Small handful fresh arugula or broccoli sprouts

Toast the bread and spread the butter on one side of each slice. Spread the guava jam over the butter, place each toast on a plate, and set aside.

Heat the oil in a medium nonstick skillet over medium heat. Crack the eggs into the skillet, cover with a tight lid, and cook until the whites are completely set but the yolks are still bright yellow and runny, 2 to 3 minutes.

Using a spatula, place two eggs on top of each slice of toast. Sprinkle with smoked paprika and season with salt and pepper. Divide the fresh arugula or sprouts evenly over the two pieces of toast and serve immediately.

BLUEBERRY BANANA RICE CAKES WITH ALMOND BUTTER

—

I keep rice cakes in the house at all times, because they're a gluten-free alternative to toast, and they make a great on-the-go breakfast. They are also a nice base for a wide variety of toppings. This recipe uses dried blueberries, which are smaller and sweeter than fresh blueberries and their texture pairs nicely with the soft banana and crunchy toast. If you can't find these in your local market or grocery store, use regular blueberries or another dried fruit of your choice. With just the right amount of protein to hold you over until lunch, this might become your favorite breakfast on fast-paced weekday mornings. Serves 1.

- 2 tablespoons almond butter

- 2 rice cakes, lightly salted

- ½ banana, thinly sliced

- 2 teaspoons honey

- ¼ teaspoon chia seeds

- 2 teaspoons dried blueberries

Spread 1 tablespoon of almond butter on one side of each rice cake. Place several slices of banana on top of the almond butter. Drizzle with about 1 teaspoon of honey and sprinkle with ⅛ teaspoon of chia seeds. Top with 1 teaspoon of dried blueberries and serve.

TOASTED BUNS WITH JAM

—

On the weekends, my dad used to make these buns on the stove for me and my brother. I hesitated (for only five seconds) to put this recipe in the book because it's almost too simple with only three ingredients, but my mouth waters just thinking about them, so I couldn't leave them out! Even though they're super easy to make, these buns are way more than the sum of their parts. Trust me when I say that this sumptuous combination tastes more delicious than toast or biscuits. You'll be using a pan on the stove to "toast" the buns instead of using a toaster oven, which gives them a buttery grilled taste. These are great to make if your kids are having their friends sleep over at your house or the grandkids are in town, or you can serve them as a breakfast side dish with the Skillet Frittata from Leftovers (page 29). Use grape jam, which is what we always had, or your own favorite flavor of jam. Serves 6 to 8.

- 3 to 4 tablespoons butter
- 1 (12-count) package sweet mini dinner rolls, such as King's Hawaiian, halved
- ½ cup grape jam

In a large nonstick pan, melt 1 tablespoon of butter over medium heat until sizzling.

Working in batches, place each roll half, cut-side down, into the pan and cook until the bottom of the bun is perfectly browned and toasted. Transfer the rolls to a platter or dish. Repeat with the remaining butter and buns. Spread approximately 1 teaspoon of jam on top of each bun and serve immediately.

ORANGE CRANBERRY FLAX MUFFINS

—

Every time I make these delicious healthy muffins, I think of my cousin Dawn, who passed away too young from breast cancer. My mother-in-law found a similar recipe in a newspaper section dedicated to breast cancer awareness month and we both found comfort in making them. These freeze well and you can thaw them one at a time as needed. My favorite way to eat them is to slice them in half, stick them under the broiler for 1 minute, and top with butter. I think they are best served warm. Makes 24 muffins.

- 2 oranges
- 1 cup all-purpose flour
- 1 cup cornmeal
- 1 cup ground flax seeds
- ½ cup oat bran

- 1 tablespoon baking powder
- 1½ cups dried cranberries
- ½ teaspoon salt
- 1 cup brown sugar

- 1 cup buttermilk
- 2 eggs
- ½ cup avocado oil
- 1 teaspoon baking soda
- ⅓ cup agave syrup

Preheat the oven to 375°F. Lightly grease two 12-cup muffin pans or use individual muffin cups.

Peel the oranges and discard the rinds. In a blender or food processor, purée the oranges until thick.

In a large bowl, combine the flour, cornmeal, flax seeds, oat bran, baking powder, cranberries, and salt and set aside.

In a medium bowl, combine the brown sugar, baking soda, buttermilk, orange pulp, eggs, oil, and agave syrup and mix well. Pour the wet ingredients into the dry ingredients and mix until well blended. The batter will be thick.

Fill the muffin cups two-thirds full and bake for 20 to 25 minutes, or until a toothpick inserted into the muffin comes out clean. Serve warm or at room temperature.

PAN-BAKED BRIOCHE FRENCH TOAST

—

The aroma of French toast throughout the house is another enticing memory that brings me back to my childhood, my grandmother's kitchen, and sleepovers. She would make my brother pancakes, and since I'm a French toast girl at heart, she would make a special batch just for me. She made hers in a skillet, but I adapted this recipe to serve a family or a small brunch crowd by using a baking sheet. This method allows for all the French toast to be completed at the same time, so you can spend less time in front of the stove and more time with your loved ones. I've used oat milk here, but you could substitute whole milk or another plant-based milk instead. Serve with a side of bacon and mixed berries for an easy, yet elegant, breakfast. Serves 4.

- 4 eggs
- ¾ cup oat milk
- 1 teaspoon vanilla extract
- 1 teaspoon ground cinnamon

- ½ teaspoon salt
- 8 thick slices brioche bread
- 1 cup pure maple syrup, warmed
- Powdered sugar, for dusting (optional)

Preheat the oven to 450°F. Place a 13-by-18-inch baking sheet in the oven while the oven is preheating.

In a shallow dish, whisk together the eggs, milk, vanilla, cinnamon, and salt until well combined.

Using an oven mitt, remove the baking sheet from the oven. Working quickly, spray the sheet liberally with nonstick cooking spray. Dip each slice of bread in the egg mixture until coated evenly on each side. Carefully place each slice on the hot baking sheet. The pan will be hot, so the bread will make a sizzling sound. Using the oven mitt, return the pan to the oven and bake for ten minutes. Serve immediately with warmed maple syrup. Dust with powdered sugar, if desired.

APPETIZERS & SNACKS

GUACAMOLE WITH TOMATO AND FETA

—

This is not your average guacamole, which is why I am asked to bring it to family functions more often than not. I'm big on textures as well as taste, and I've always thought traditional guacamole didn't have an appealing consistency or the most interesting flavor. The feta crumbles and chopped tomato in this recipe add a chunky texture that will leave people asking, "What's in here?" which has turned this dip into the ultimate chip-scooping, crowd-pleasing favorite. I like to double this recipe and use the extra as a base for Avocado Toast Two Ways (page 35). Serves 4 to 6.

- 2 ripe avocados

- Zest and juice of 1 lime (see Tip)

- 1 tablespoon olive oil

- ¼ cup crumbled feta

- 5 grape tomatoes, chopped

- 1 tablespoon chopped fresh cilantro (see Tip)

- ¼ teaspoon salt

- Tortilla chips, for serving

Cut the avocados in half and remove the pits. Scoop out the flesh into a small bowl. Add the lime zest and juice and the olive oil. Use the back of a spoon to press and rotate the mixture until it has a smooth, creamy texture. Add the feta, tomatoes, cilantro, and salt and gently stir until combined. Serve at room temperature with tortilla chips on the side.

 Tip: For all you essential oil fans, as an alternative to the lime juice and zest, you can use 2 drops of food-quality lime essential oil and 1 drop of cilantro oil instead of the fresh lime and herbs.

Mexican Medley Menu

GUACAMOLE WITH TOMATO AND FETA (page 49)

TORTILLA CHIPS AND SALSA

CILANTRO LIME ROCK SHRIMP TACOS (page 100)

THE BEST SKINNY MARGARITAS (page 202)

—

SET THE SCENE

To add an embellishing twist to Taco Tuesday, create a digital menu that you can text to your guests for this summery Mexican medley by using a fun background photograph of a cactus or a sliced-open avocado on your cutting board.

Make the guacamole ahead of time but the same day (guacamole does not store well over time), cover, and refrigerate. Stir just before serving. Make the margaritas in a pitcher ahead of time, refrigerate, and add ice just before serving.

Create a taco bar of toppings in small bowls or ramekins on the dining table with some of your favorites, such as salsa, chopped green chiles, sliced jalapeños, black beans, and extra Mexican Cotija cheese.

MEDITERRANEAN HUMMUS DIP

—

There are lots of great hummus varieties in grocery stores these days, but in my opinion, serving it straight out of the container has lost its luster. Because I believe the texture of food is a big part of its tastiness, I love adding chopped fresh Mediterranean-inspired ingredients to store-bought hummus, which adds to its deliciousness. Hearty, healthy, and creamy, this dip will be what you have in mind when you ask your host, "Can I bring something?" Serves 6 to 8.

- 1 (8-ounce) container plain hummus
- 1½ cups plain low-fat Greek yogurt
- 1 cup chopped fresh spinach
- ½ cup roasted red peppers, drained and chopped
- ½ cup marinated artichoke hearts, drained and chopped
- ½ cup pitted and sliced kalamata olives
- ½ cup sliced scallions
- ½ cup crumbled feta cheese
- Pita chips, for serving

In a small bowl, combine the hummus, yogurt, spinach, red peppers, artichoke hearts, olives, scallions, and feta cheese and stir until well mixed. Serve with pita chips.

SINFULLY SUPREME PIZZA DIP

—

A pizza you can dip into? Yes, please! This recipe has been around for such a long time in our family that no one can recall when or where it actually originated. But it is, without a doubt, the most popular appetizer ever served at our family gatherings. It's delicious and easy and can even be doubled for a larger gathering or a crowd on game nights. I like to buy the "scooped" varieties of corn chips that you can find in the store, such as Fritos Scoops, because they are more durable for the thick consistency of this dip. Trust me when I say that you'll pass this recipe along to all your friends every time you serve it. Make it "supreme" or customize it with your favorite pizza toppings. Serves 8 to 10.

- 1 (8-ounce) package light cream cheese, at room temperature

- 1 (13-ounce) jar pizza sauce

- 2 cups shredded mozzarella cheese

- ¼ cup pepperoni slices, halved, or mini pepperoni bites

- ¼ cup chopped white mushrooms

- ¼ cup sliced black olives

- ¼ cup chopped green bell pepper

- Sturdy corn chips, for serving

Preheat the oven to 350°F.

Working in layers, spread the cream cheese evenly on the bottom of a round pie plate or casserole dish. Spread the pizza sauce over the cream cheese. Sprinkle the shredded mozzarella over the top and finish with the pepperoni, mushrooms, black olives, and bell peppers.

Bake for 15 minutes. Switch the oven to a high broil and broil for 2 to 3 minutes, or until the cheese is golden brown and crispy around the edges. Serve hot with tortilla chips.

 Tip: If you're transporting this appetizer, bake it but leave the broiling for when you arrive at your destination. Cover the pan with foil and place it in a heat-safe carrier. When you arrive, remove the foil and broil until golden brown and slightly bubbly, 2 to 3 minutes.

MINI HOT DOG WRAPS WITH PEACH MUSTARD SAUCE

—

Whether you're hosting a black-tie affair or a family movie night, this classic hors d'oeuvre must be invited. The sweet and spicy peach mustard sauce gives traditional "pigs in a blanket" a modern twist on the taste buds. Make these ahead of time, store them in the fridge, and pop them in the oven just before serving. Serves 8 to 10.

- 2 (8-ounce) cans refrigerated crescent rolls, such as Pillsbury
- 1 (14-ounce) package mini beef hot dogs, such as Hillshire Farm Beef Lit'l Smokies
- ¼ cup spicy brown mustard
- 2 tablespoons peach jelly

Preheat the oven to 375°F. Line a baking sheet with parchment paper.

Remove the crescent rolls from the can and unroll them on a cutting board. Using the perforations in the dough as a guide, separate the dough into triangles. Cut each triangle in half again, making two smaller triangles. Place one hot dog at the tip of each triangle and roll it in the dough, pressing gently at the ends to seal.

Place each wrapped hot dog on the baking sheet, making sure to keep them about 1 inch apart. Bake for 12 to 15 minutes, or until golden brown.

In a small bowl, whisk together the brown mustard and peach jelly until combined.

Transfer the wraps to a serving platter and serve with the sauce for dipping.

Game Day Menu

SINFULLY SUPREME PIZZA DIP (page 52)

MINI HOT DOG WRAPS WITH PEACH MUSTARD SAUCE (page 54)

VEGGIE TRAY

CHICKEN WINGS WITH BLUE CHEESE OR RANCH DRESSING

CRISPY RICE OATMEAL CHOCOLATE CHIP COOKIES (page 175)

—

SET THE SCENE

Buy a premade, store-bought veggie and dip tray. Make the cookies the day before. Prepare the pizza dip and hot dog wraps the day before or the day of and refrigerate. Bake the pizza dip first, and then bake the hot dog wraps. Just before serving, set the pizza dip under the broiler to finish it off.

Set the wings on a large platter. In mason jars or ramekins, serve a selection of dipping sauces, such as blue cheese or ranch dressing.

Purchase fun sports-themed napkins and heavy-duty paper food trays from a party store or online for easy and mess-free serving. These are great to have on hand for occasions when people are eating around a couch or standing up.

Keep drinks simple and try to avoid glassware, as people tend to get rowdy and fingers get saucy! Stick to cans of beer, wine, and sparkling water.

WASABI DEVILED EGGS

—

Deviled eggs are another appetizer that was served at my family gatherings over the generations, most memorably by my Nana. She would make them the traditional way, with paprika sprinkled on top. Today, as queen chef of my own home, not only do I sprinkle smoked paprika on top the way Nana did, but I also add wasabi to give these spicy deviled eggs a real kick. Watch your guests come back for thirds. Try my method for easy-to-peel boiled eggs; it's practically foolproof. Serves 6 to 8.

- 8 eggs

- ½ cup light or vegan mayonnaise

- 2 teaspoons rice vinegar

- 1½ teaspoons wasabi paste

- 1 tablespoon chopped scallions

- 1 teaspoon black sesame seeds

- Smoked paprika, for sprinkling

Pour 3 inches of water into an 8-quart saucepan over medium-high heat and bring to a low steady boil, with only a few slow bubbles at the top. Using a slotted spoon, carefully place each egg into the water, making sure it does not hit the bottom with force. Let cook for 13 minutes. With the slotted spoon, remove the eggs one at a time and place them directly into a large airtight container. Seal the container and immediately place it in the fridge for at least 3 hours before peeling.

Carefully peel the shell from the eggs and rinse under cold water to remove any shell remnants. Cut the eggs in half lengthwise, which will help the eggs lie flatter. Remove the yolks with a small spoon and place them in a medium bowl. Add the mayonnaise, rice vinegar, wasabi paste, and scallions and mix until smooth and creamy.

Using a rubber spatula, transfer the yolk mixture to a large plastic bag and seal out all of the air. Gently squeeze the mixture to one corner of the bag, and cut about ½ inch off the corner. Fill the egg whites by gently squeezing the bag and using a swirling motion to pipe the egg yolk mixture decoratively to just over the top of the cavity. Top with the sesame seeds and a sprinkle of smoked paprika to taste.

Arrange the deviled eggs on a serving platter and refrigerate for at least 30 minutes before serving.

WATERMELON, FETA, AND MINT SKEWERS

—

Skewers aren't just for cooking meat and veggies on the grill. They also work really well for displaying these two-bite appetizers that are as beautiful to serve as they are refreshing to eat. I love the combination of sweet watermelon, salty feta, and cool mint, and I use this trio often in salads. Using a whole watermelon ensures that you'll get exactly the cube sizes you want, but sometimes I start with precut watermelon from the store when I'm short on time. Use short bamboo skewers and serve these as a decorative tailgate party appetizer or as an addition to a charcuterie board for a barbecue. Serves 10 to 12.

- 1 (3-pound) watermelon

- 1 to 2 teaspoons fresh lime juice

- 1 (8-ounce) block feta cheese

- 24 fresh mint leaves

Cut the rind and white part off the sides of the watermelon and discard. Cut the watermelon into 25 (1-inch) cubes. Discard any seeds. Drizzle the lime juice evenly over the watermelon cubes. Cut the feta into 25 (¾-inch) cubes.

Using a bamboo skewer, thread a watermelon cube, a mint leaf, a chunk of feta, another mint leaf, and another piece of watermelon. Thread the last piece of watermelon only partly on the skewer so it forms a base that can stand upright on a serving plate. Repeat with the rest of the skewers and ingredients and arrange them on the serving plate. Serve immediately or chilled.

PROTEIN-PACKED GRANOLA BARS

—

I gotta admit, I am slightly famous around town for these granola bars. I love to exercise in the mornings and sometimes I don't want to eat breakfast before a workout. These make the perfect snack to grab on the go. As the name promises, they are packed with protein and they taste more like a dessert than a snack. They've received rave reviews from my tribe of active friends and family, so I keep a big batch of them in a glass storage container in the fridge, which is enough for about a week of individual snacks. Makes 30 to 40.

- 1 cup natural peanut butter
- 1 cup natural almond butter
- 3 cups granola
- 1 cup chocolate chips
- 1 cup dried cranberries
- 1 cup toasted coconut chips

- 1 cup toasted coconut flakes
- ½ cup sliced almonds
- ¼ cup chia seeds
- ¼ cup honey
- 1 teaspoon ground cinnamon
- 1 teaspoon coarse sea salt

Line a 9-by-13-inch baking dish with 1-inch sides with parchment paper.

In a large bowl, mix together the peanut butter and almond butter with a spatula until well blended. Add the granola, chocolate chips, dried cranberries, coconut chips, coconut flakes, almonds, chia seeds, honey, cinnamon, and sea salt and mix until combined.

Transfer the mixture to the baking dish and with your hands press it evenly all the way to the edges of the dish to about ½ inch thick. Refrigerate for at least 2 hours.

Using a sharp knife, cut into 1-by-2-inch bars. The bars can be stored in an airtight container in the refrigerator for up to 1 week.

CHARCUTERIE BOARDS

While *charcuterie* is an old French word that literally means an arrangement of different cured meats, the modern-day charcuterie board has turned into a fancy and trendy way of serving food of all kinds to many people in one setting. It's another way to bring people together, through gathering close with good conversation and creative food pairings.

Charcuterie

Charcuterie is typically served on a wooden board of some sort and includes an assortment of various cured meats, cheeses, dried fruit, nuts, crackers, and jams. Some people take the term *charcuterie board* well beyond its literal meaning and include other paired combinations of food, such as fast food or desserts. It can really be whatever you want it to be.

I have really grown to love the art of arranging food, and creating charcuterie boards was the genesis of that passion. For those who feel less confident in their creativity, rest assured that there are no culinary skills required here, nor is there one right or wrong way to assemble a beautiful board. But you can follow some of the great guidelines in this chapter and use them as inspiration to make a charcuterie board assembly that is doable and beautiful.

BOARDS AND SURFACES

If you don't have a large wooden board or butcher block, no worries! A large platter works or any portable surface that is aesthetically pleasing, such as a marble cutting board or a long porcelain platter. Discount home goods stores sell inexpensive boards, which makes it possible to have an assortment of shapes and sizes on hand. You can even lay a large sheet of butcher paper across your table or countertop and use that as the base to create a charcuterie assortment. That idea works best for larger crowds or when you want to serve charcuterie as dinner instead of a lighter snack. I've seen this work on kitchen islands where people can move around the table on all sides and it can be highly effective. Charcuterie does not need to be limited to boards for arranging your coordinating foods. All you need is a vessel of some kind, and I've made them using small crates or baskets.

MEATS AND CHEESES

I like to use a variety of cured meats that run the gamut of preparation styles. Sliced prosciutto looks beautiful when placed imperfectly in little piles, and cured sausages such as salami, chorizo, and pepperoni present beautifully in a domino arrangement. There are great references on the Internet and in design forums such as Pinterest, where you can find clever ways to display cured meats in the shape of flowers using household items such as a wineglass for guidelines. Place pâté in small glass bowls or ramekins.

Cheese assortments make a board more interesting, so when deciding on what to present, be sure to use at least two of the following categories: aged, soft, firm, or blue. My favorite aged cheeses are Cheddar and Gouda. Soft cheeses such as Brie and Gournay make good spreads. When it comes to firm cheeses, I love to serve Parmigiano-Reggiano or Manchego, and Gorgonzola makes a great option for blue cheese. Use a different knife for each cheese, and try to arrange hard meats next to hard cheeses, because they both require similar knives for slicing. When it comes to an assortment of meats and cheeses, small, handwritten labels are a fun and creative way to let your guests know what they're eating.

ACCOMPANIMENTS

It's nice to add other complementary items to enhance your board's food theme, and there are so many things to choose from. Some accompaniments for a traditional board are crackers, sliced bread, nuts, jams, honey, dips, chips, fresh or dried fruit, pickles, olives, and peppers. No matter what you choose, one general rule of thumb is to use quality ingredients and choose foods that are presentable—they need to look good. For example, nuts like Marcona almonds, cashews, and walnuts present better than peanuts and pistachios. Dips such as hummus and salsa make nice accompaniments and are great alternatives to spreadable cheeses. Jams and honey should make an appearance for a nice spreadable accompaniment to cheese. For these, I keep an assortment of small glass bowls and ramekins on hand, as well as a honey wand and mini spoons for serving.

PRESENTATION

Arrangement and organization are key elements to presenting a beautiful charcuterie board that doesn't resemble a pile of food rubble.

Go big first.

I like to place larger items on the board first, such as blocks of cheese or a bowl with dip. Spread out these larger items so that it creates a visual balance. Next, place the remaining cheeses and meats around the board, leaving space for crackers and accompaniments. Fill in any blank spaces with crackers, nuts, fresh and dried fruit, jams, honey, or chocolate. Berries also make great fillers for larger boards that often have lots of space to fill.

Use different shapes and angles.

As you'll see on the following pages, I love to arrange cheese and crackers at different angles. For example, if I'm using breadsticks, I'll lay one stack one way and another stack a different way on the other side of the board. Most people think to place sliced cheese or meats in layers, but it also looks interesting if you turn them around and stack them at different angles. It's also a clever idea to present the same fresh fruits and vegetables in different forms. For example, serve slices of dried mango next to a whole, unopened mango or sliced grape tomatoes next to a larger tomato. Playing around with shapes, textures, and colors of food is all part of the adventure!

Add dimension.

Varying the heights of all the elements makes for a beautiful presentation, especially on larger boards. A taller glass is a nice holder for breadsticks and a martini glass makes for an interesting display for nuts and chocolates. I have a cabinet in my garage specifically for storing my charcuterie boards, and I also store various glasses and containers I've picked up from discount home goods stores, thrift stores, and awesome sales.

Fill in the blanks.

After you've placed your meats, cheeses, and accompaniments on the board, you will inevitably have holes to fill. It is not necessary to fill in these holes on small, simple boards, but larger boards will need some love. This is where you will find a home for the smaller nuts and berries, as well as flowers.

Arrange flowers.

Yes! Flowers are my favorite addition to an edible canvas. Some markets sell small edible flowers, which are a great addition, but mostly I use larger, nonedible flowers, such as a few roses left over from my arrangements, to complete my charcuterie boards. I've also formed entire boards around beautiful flowers that catch my eye, such as the purple roses in the Board for a Crowd (page 70). You cannot go wrong with this elegant touch on your board.

THEMES

The latest trends in charcuterie themes run the gamut of seasons, geographic regions, food genres, color palettes, and holidays, just to mention a few. I've served taco boards, burger boards, dessert boards, and even kid-friendly boards. Once, for a burger cookout, I composed a large rimmed circular board with handles filled only with different forms of potatoes, such as French fries and tater tots with varieties of sweet and white potatoes. Nestled in between were condiments in small bowls. The possibilities are endless!

BOARD FOR A CROWD

Large boards are a great way to prepare an appetizer without having to cook. Better yet, using what you have in your kitchen to assemble a last-minute assortment will make you look like a rock star.

The most important thing to remember here is that you don't need to be as creative as you do intentional. Begin by imagining one or two items you'd like to feature on your board, such as a fruit in season or your favorite cheese. It could even be the beautiful blooming roses on your dining room table. That was the case when I assembled the board pictured here. I had gone to the flower market a few days before and these purple roses caught my eye. As I imagined creating a charcuterie board, I knew I wanted to keep the color palette warm and soft, playing off of the pale purple roses and capturing the season of fall. I grabbed pitted prunes and dark purple grapes and trimmed some lavender from the garden. Then I grabbed pears, kiwi, and green tomatoes to balance the color wheel.

Think about the technique I mentioned about the placement of crackers and breadsticks for an interesting layout. Lay out your largest items first—usually cheeses and meats—followed by crackers, and then fill in holes with the accompaniments. Flowers and herbs always go last. You'll want to trim the roses or other flowers almost to the blossom and nestle them among items so they face upward. I like to lay herbs, such as rosemary or thyme, flat on the board so they hang off the edge a bit, which makes for a nice visual touch. You don't always need to stay in the parameters of the board or vessel you're using. If you're refrigerating the board, keep the flowers and herbs off until you're ready to serve.

Luncheon for a Shower Menu

MIMOSAS

BOARD FOR A CROWD (page 70)

WASABI DEVILED EGGS (page 56)

CHICKEN SALAD

CROISSANTS

PEAR GORGONZOLA SALAD (page 89)

ORANGE CRANBERRY FLAX MUFFINS (page 42)

—

SET THE SCENE

Buy premade chicken salad from your favorite deli and croissants to serve it on. Make the Orange Cranberry Flax Muffins the day before and store in an airtight container. Boil the eggs for the Wasabi Deviled Eggs the day before, storing the yolk mixture and egg whites separately in the fridge and assembling the day of.

Decide on a color theme for your board and choose foods and flowers to complement the theme.

Serve fruit-infused water in glass pitchers to be poured into pastel water goblets.

Use small bud vase flower and herb arrangements with handwritten tags as place settings for take-home gifts.

SIMPLE BOARD

———————

One of my husband's favorite quotes is from Leonardo da Vinci: "Simplicity is the ultimate sophistication." My husband is a minimalist by nature and in his architectural designs he is always careful to allow each space to breathe, revealing its true beauty. This is the root of the Modern Hippie way of life; it's about finding a "new" way to bring back the "old," simple version of life. It comes out in the way I present my food, and a small board is no exception.

A simple charcuterie board is my favorite way to recognize the beauty of food arranging. It's ideal to serve at a quick cocktail hour before you run out to dinner with friends. You'll want to select a beautiful marble or wood surface to channel your inner da Vinci. Choose one cheese, one meat, sliced bread instead of crackers, and always some sort of garnish of fresh herbs.

A simple board is ideal for a picnic because it's easy to transport and set up. A picnic for two at sunset on the beach—that's my idea of a perfect end to the day. Transport that simple charcuterie board in the back of your car or the basket of your bike and tote a cooler of wine.

On one of our recent beach outings, we picked up a discarded piece of old wooden fence from the neighborhood to serve as a table for our picnic. It's a good idea to have some sort of a sturdy surface other than your picnic blanket to rest the food and wine on.

Date Night In Menu

A BOTTLE OF YOUR FAVORITE WINE

SIMPLE BOARD (page 72)

TOSSED GREEN SALAD WITH LEMON ROMANO VINAIGRETTE
(page 91)

CHRISTIAN'S CLASSIC ITALIAN PASTA (page 116)

CHOCOLATE-COVERED STRAWBERRIES

—

SET THE SCENE

Start the mood out right by making a day out of the experience. Go together to a fancier market than your local grocery store or divide and conquer the tasks. One person can be in charge of shopping for food and the other for a nice bottle of Italian red wine. Buy premade chocolate-covered strawberries or another dessert of your choice.

Arrange the simple charcuterie board and make the dessert ahead of time, so that you can spend time cooking the pasta dish *together* as part of your date night experience.

Since it's just the two of you, make it special by using your finest tableware. Rather than one larger vase of flowers, take a more intimate approach and use votive candleholders—one in front of each plate—as small vases with three to five roses cut so that just the blossoms stick out at the top. Stick in some leftover basil leaves from your pasta ingredients for a touch of complementary green.

Dim the lights before you start to cook the meal together, so that several small strategically scattered votive candles are the main light source at the table. Soft jazz is my favorite date music, and when it's my turn to pick, I particularly love playing jazz saxophonist Stan Getz on the record player. Make a deal to talk about goals, dreams, and ideas over your meal.

SWEET DESSERT BOARD

One of my favorite ways to play with food is to build a themed board, and desserts are always my theme of choice! It's a good idea to pick a featured dessert theme, such as donuts or cake bites, and build from there. I knew in advance that I wanted to make chocolate donuts with pink icing, and I wanted to use pink rose petals as an accent. My Vegan Chocolate Donuts with Strawberry Icing (page 181) steal the show when I serve them, so naturally they make a great dessert to feature. When I was at the grocery store, I bought other sweet items that fit in with the color palette of purples, pinks, and chocolate. Berries are the easiest way to add some healthy options for people who may not eat gluten or chocolate, and they're great for filling in those holes.

Think about shapes as you shop for ingredients. Donuts, roses, and macarons are round, so I added in some biscotti and pirouette cookies for some longer shapes and some cream-filled wafers for squares.

Roses on dessert boards are a must. They're a reminder to take in the small, beautiful things in life and indulge in the moment, though feel free to use whatever flowers you like best. If you're buying flowers to arrange, set a few aside—I like to use a combination of big and small—and cut them right at the base of the blossom, then nestle them into the small gaps.

SALADS

WEDGE SALAD LETTUCE CUPS

—

I love a good wedge, but here's the thing—it's usually served as one-quarter of a head of iceberg lettuce and it can be cumbersome to cut. I think a wedge salad served as individual lettuce leaves is not only more presentable, but it also makes it easier to cut with a fork and knife. To make this quick and easy, you can use my favorite healthier store-bought ranch dressing, Bolthouse Farms Classic Ranch Yogurt Dressing, which you can find in the refrigerated section of the grocery store. This salad looks as beautiful on the serving platter as it tastes on the palate. Serves 4 to 6.

- 2 heads romaine lettuce

- 12 ounces tricolored grape tomatoes, halved

- 8 ounces cooked bacon or turkey bacon, cut into small pieces

- ⅓ cup ranch dressing

- 2 ounces crumbled blue cheese

- Black pepper

Wash the romaine under running water and pat dry with paper towels. Cut approximately 2 inches off the bottom of each head. Separate the individual lettuce leaves and place them on a large serving platter, placing the larger leaves on the bottom and stacking some of the smaller leaves inside the larger ones. Each lettuce cup will be one serving. Place the tomatoes evenly among the lettuce cups. Sprinkle the bacon over the lettuce cups. Drizzle the dressing and scatter the blue cheese over the top. Season with black pepper to taste and serve.

NOT YOUR AVERAGE CAESAR SALAD

—

Some people don't like Caesar salads because they have anchovies, but in this Caesar, you don't need them to enjoy its classic flavors. It's served in a nontraditional way on individual romaine lettuce leaves, which makes it easier to eat with a fork and knife and gives it a beautiful and elegant appearance on your table. I've used my favorite vinaigrette here and the recipe makes plenty to store in the fridge for salads in the future. If you do not have a mason jar, use a small bowl and whisk until combined. Serves 4.

- ½ cup gluten-free bread crumbs

- 1 heart of romaine

- ¼ cup fresh mint leaves, roughly torn

- Lemon Romano Vinaigrette (page 91)

- ¼ cup grated Parmesan cheese

In a small pan over medium heat, toast the bread crumbs, stirring often to keep them from burning, until fragrant, 2 to 3 minutes. Set aside to cool.

Cut about 2 inches off the stalk of the romaine. Separate the individual lettuce leaves and place them on a large serving platter, placing the larger leaves first and stacking some of the smaller leaves inside the larger ones. Scatter the torn mint on top of the lettuce. Pour the desired amount of dressing over top of the lettuce, carefully coating each leaf. Scatter the bread crumbs over the top, followed by the Parmesan cheese. Serve at room temperature or cold.

WINTER BERRY SALAD

—

Ripe berries, candied pecans, and Gorgonzola cheese combine to make this edible artwork a family favorite. The decorative presentation of the berries and the taste of candied cinnamon pecans reminds me of Christmas. Each time I make this salad, I am also reminded of my sister-in-law, Megan, who introduced it to our family years ago. Serves 4 to 6.

- I cup pecans
- ¼ cup pure maple syrup
- ¼ teaspoon ground cinnamon
- I (5-ounce) package mixed greens
- I cup raspberries
- I cup strawberries, stems removed and quartered
- I cup blackberries

- ½ cup olive oil
- 2 tablespoons balsamic vinegar
- I tablespoon Dijon mustard
- I tablespoon honey
- ¼ teaspoon salt
- ¼ cup crumbled Gorgonzola cheese

Line a baking sheet with parchment paper.

In a small sauté pan over medium-low heat, combine the pecans, maple syrup, and cinnamon and cook, stirring constantly, until the syrup starts to crystallize and sticks to the nuts, 5 to 7 minutes. Transfer the glazed pecans to the prepared baking sheet and spread them out in an even layer. Let cool completely.

In a large salad bowl, combine the greens, raspberries, strawberries, and blackberries and toss gently until combined.

In a small bowl, whisk together the olive oil, balsamic vinegar, mustard, honey, and salt. Pour the dressing over the salad and toss gently until coated well. Top with the candied pecans and Gorgonzola cheese and serve at room temperature or chilled.

MANDARIN ORANGE AND RED ONION SALAD

—

My mother-in-law, Janice, has inspired me to experiment with making my own salads and dressings. She would make salads according to the seasons and what was ripe at that time. This Floridian summer salad is one of her creations, and it pairs best with red meat. You'll love the way the toasted almonds taste with the sweet mandarin oranges and the tangy homemade dressing. I prefer to use fresh orange segments, but to save time you can use one 11-ounce can of mandarin oranges, drained. Serves 4 to 6.

- ½ cup plus 1 teaspoon avocado oil, divided

- 1 cup sliced almonds

- 2 large or 3 medium heads romaine lettuce

- 2 small mandarin or clementine oranges, peeled

- 1 small red onion, thinly sliced

- 2 tablespoons fresh lemon juice

- ½ teaspoon sugar

- ½ teaspoon salt

- ¼ teaspoon white pepper

In a small pan over medium heat, warm 1 teaspoon of the avocado oil. Add the sliced almonds and cook, stirring often, until toasted, about 5 minutes. Set aside to cool.

Cut about 2 inches off the bottom of each head of romaine. Chop the leaves into 1-inch sections. Separate the segments of the oranges. In a large salad bowl, combine the lettuce, orange segments, and onion slices.

In a separate small bowl, whisk together the lemon juice, sugar, salt, white pepper, and remaining ½ cup of avocado oil. Pour the dressing over the salad and toss until well combined. Sprinkle the toasted almonds over the top and serve at room temperature or chilled.

PEACH, MINT, AND FETA SALAD

—

I have a real love affair with fresh herbs in salads. Adding in the cool taste of mint gives this salad a brighter, earthy taste. In Florida it always feels like summer, and this combination of juicy ripe peaches, feta, and herbs is one of my all-time favorite summer salads, so we eat it a lot. It is important to have perfectly ripe peaches so you get all the juicy flavorful benefits. Serves 4 to 6.

- 5 ounces arugula

- 3 ripe peaches, pitted and slice

- I handful fresh mint, roughly torn

- ¾ cup crumbled feta cheese

- ⅓ cup sliced almonds, toasted

- ⅓ cup olive oil

- 3 tablespoons lemon juice

- 2 tablespoons red wine vinegar

- I teaspoon honey

- ½ teaspoon salt

In a large salad bowl, combine the arugula, peaches, mint, feta, and almonds.

In a small bowl, whisk together the olive oil, lemon juice, vinegar, honey, and salt until well combined. Pour the dressing over the salad and toss gently. Serve immediately.

Summer Nights

FRESH GRAPEFRUIT PALOMAS (page 194)

PEACH, MINT, AND FETA SALAD (page 86)

ROSEMARY ONION MAC AND CHEESE (page 161)

TENDER, CRISPY BARBECUE RIBS (page 133)

—

SET THE SCENE

Prepare the Palomas ahead of time and store the mixture in a pitcher without ice in the fridge. Make the mac and cheese ahead of time and bake just before serving. Bake the ribs a few hours before company arrives and place on the grill just before serving.

While the grill is heating up and the sun is going down, choose a music playlist of good vibrations. Create your own playlist of your favorite upbeat hits or queue up a premade list from the Internet.

Simplistic elegance can be achieved by keeping the color palette simple, such as classic red, white, or navy, and by replacing plastic with wooden cutlery. Display the cutlery in mason jars or small metal buckets lined with butcher or parchment paper.

Mason jars also work well as vases for displaying simple arrangements of sunflowers, white mums, or basic greenery from around your yard as part of your table decor.

Use a burlap runner or a fabric tablecloth with a casual feel, such as a vintage-looking bed sheet. Dark-colored cloth napkins work best for sticky barbecue fingers.

PEAR GORGONZOLA SALAD

—

Here is another salad recipe inspired by my mother-in-law, one that we always used to make with Harry & David pears. These pears are truly the best and can be purchased online and shipped to your door from August to October, when they are in season. But your local grocery store pears will do just fine. You'll want to choose soft, ripe pears, as their sweet juiciness complements the full-flavored, salty Gorgonzola. This is a lovely fall salad that pairs well with red meat, poultry, or fish. Serves 6.

- ⅓ cup olive oil

- 2 tablespoons sherry or white wine vinegar

- 4 teaspoons honey

- 1 tablespoon Dijon mustard

- ¼ teaspoons salt

- 1 small head radicchio lettuce, chopped

- 2 heads Bibb or butter lettuce, torn into small pieces

- 2 large ripe pears, such as Bosc, Bartlett, or Anjou, cored and cut into ½-inch cubes

- ¾ cup crumbled Gorgonzola cheese

- Black pepper

In a small bowl, whisk together the oil, vinegar, honey, mustard, and salt. Set aside.

In a medium salad bowl, combine the radicchio, Bibb lettuce, pears, cheese, and dressing and toss gently. Season with black pepper to taste and serve.

WILD SALMON SALAD

—

Wild-caught salmon is one of the healthiest sources of omega-3 fatty acids and is packed with vitamins. I prefer its milder taste and health benefits over canned tuna. This was my daily lunch when I did a metabolic detox cleanse a while back and I felt so good after I ate it that I still keep all the ingredients on hand to make this quick and delicious lunch. I serve the salmon salad over a bed of lettuce and fresh chopped veggies with crispy chow mein noodles and drizzle it with a delicious sesame ginger dressing. Serves 2.

- 2 (6-ounce) cans wild Alaskan salmon, drained

- 2 heads romaine lettuce

- ⅔ cup shredded carrots

- ⅔ cup chopped snap peas

- ⅓ cup chopped scallions

- 1 cup Sesame Ginger Dressing (page 91)

- 1 cup chow mein noodles

In a medium bowl, use a fork to break up the salmon into small pieces.

Cut 1 inch off the top leafy part of the romaine and about 2 inches off the bottom. Chop the romaine into 1-inch pieces.

In a medium serving bowl, combine the lettuce, salmon, carrots, snap peas, and scallions. Pour the dressing over the salad and toss gently until well combined. Top with the chow mein noodles and serve.

MASON JAR SALAD DRESSING THREE WAYS

—

Mason jars serve many purposes in my home, from vases to craft storage to salad dressing containers. Once you see how easy it is to make salad dressings in a mason jar, you won't even be tempted to go back to store-bought dressings, which are full of unhealthy oils, sugars, and preservatives. I usually keep a jar of the Lemon Romano Vinaigrette in the fridge as my go-to salad dressing, so that recipe yields more than the others. I also use it as a marinade for chicken and for a delicious dip for pizza (oh yes, I sure do!). For each of these dressings, simply combine the ingredients in a 16-ounce mason jar and shake well. Serve immediately or store in the fridge for up to 1 week.

Lemon Romano Vinaigrette (makes 1⅓ cups)

- ⅔ cup olive oil
- ⅓ cup champagne vinegar
- ¼ cup fresh lemon juice
- 1½ tablespoons Dijon mustard
- ⅔ cup grated Pecorino Romano cheese
- 1 garlic clove, minced
- 1 teaspoon salt
- 1 teaspoon black pepper

Sesame Ginger Dressing (makes 1 cup)

- ½ cup avocado oil
- ¼ cup tamari or soy sauce
- ¼ cup honey
- 2 tablespoons rice vinegar
- 1½ tablespoons fresh lemon juice
- 2 teaspoons sesame oil
- 2 teaspoons black sesame seeds
- 1 teaspoon grated ginger

Honey Mustard Dressing (makes ⅔ cup)

- ¼ cup olive oil
- ¼ cup Dijon mustard
- 3 tablespoons apple cider vinegar
- 3 tablespoons honey
- ½ teaspoon salt

MAIN DISHES

ROASTED VEGGIE QUINOA BOWLS

—

This colorful protein-packed bowl of goodness will satisfy meat lovers and vegans alike. Roasted chickpeas and sweet potatoes combined with a tangy Asian-inspired carrot-ginger dressing make this savory bowl a real comfort craving. Feel free to switch up the veggies and proteins as you please. Serves 4.

For the bowls:

- 2 cups tricolored quinoa, rinsed

- 1 (15-ounce) can chickpeas, drained and rinsed

- 1 large sweet potato, peeled and cut into 1-inch cubes

- 2 tablespoons olive oil

- ½ teaspoon salt

- 1 (15-ounce) can fire-roasted corn

- 1 cup shredded red cabbage

- 1 cup canned black beans, drained and rinsed

- 4 medium radishes, trimmed and thinly sliced

- 2 medium avocados, pitted, peeled, and thinly sliced

- Torn fresh cilantro, for garnish

For the carrot ginger dressing:

- ⅓ cup olive oil

- ⅓ cup rice vinegar

- 3 carrots, peeled and chopped

- 2 tablespoons peeled and chopped ginger

- 2 tablespoons fresh lime juice

- 1½ tablespoons honey

- 1 teaspoon toasted sesame oil

To make the bowl:

Preheat the oven to 425°F. Line a baking sheet with parchment paper.

In a 4-quart saucepan, combine the quinoa and 4 cups of water and bring to a boil over high heat. Turn the heat down to a low simmer, cover, and cook until

Continued

the grains are translucent, about 15 minutes. Remove from the heat and let cool, uncovered.

Place the chickpeas on a paper towel and pat dry. Place the sweet potato cubes and chickpeas on the prepared baking sheet and toss with the olive oil and salt. Bake until the sweet potatoes are soft and the chickpeas are toasted and golden brown, about 30 minutes.

To make the dressing:

Combine the olive oil, rice vinegar, carrots, ginger, lime juice, honey, and sesame oil in a blender and blend until smooth.

To assemble:

Spoon 1 cup of the quinoa into each of 4 bowls as a base. Divide the sweet potatoes, chickpeas, corn, cabbage, radish slices, black beans, and avocado slices evenly among the bowls, arranging them decoratively.

Pour ¼ to ½ cup of dressing over each bowl, top with the torn cilantro, and serve warm or at room temperature

TOFU AND VEGGIE FRIED RICE

—

If I see a lonely white onion or an abundance of cooked rice stored in my fridge that's not being used, this fried rice dish is the first thing that comes to mind. It's a fun challenge for me to make a meal around what I already have in the fridge and pantry. Veggie fried rice does double duty as a meal or a side dish, but when you add crispy tofu, it gives you a low-fat, high-fiber protein that creates a completely balanced meal. I like using tamari as an alternative to soy sauce because it's gluten-free and has a deeper flavor. Serves 4 to 6.

- 14 ounces extra-firm tofu

- 4 tablespoons avocado oil, divided

- 2 tablespoons sesame oil, divided

- 4 tablespoons hoisin sauce, divided

- 1 medium white onion, diced

- 2 garlic cloves, minced

- 2 cups chopped shiitake mushrooms

- 1 cup shredded carrots

- 1 cup frozen green peas, thawed

- 1 teaspoon salt

- 6 cups cooked white rice

- 6 tablespoons tamari or soy sauce

Slice the tofu block in half and press the pieces between folded paper towels until it feels mostly dry to the touch. Cut the pieces into 1-inch cubes.

Line a plate with paper towels.

In a 12-inch nonstick skillet over medium-high heat, heat 2 tablespoons of the avocado oil, 1 tablespoon of the sesame oil, and 1 tablespoon of the hoisin sauce. Add the tofu and cook, tossing often, until crispy on all sides, about 20 minutes. Using a slotted spoon, transfer the tofu to the paper towel–lined plate.

In an 8-quart pot over medium heat, heat the remaining 2 tablespoons of avocado oil. Add the onion and garlic and sauté until soft, about 3 minutes. Add the mushrooms, carrots, peas, and salt and sauté, stirring often, for an additional 5 minutes. Turn the heat to low, add the cooked rice, tamari, and remaining 3 table-spoons of hoisin sauce and 1 tablespoon of sesame oil and cook, stirring often, until heated through, 3 to 5 minutes.

CILANTRO LIME ROCK SHRIMP TACOS

—

Taco 'bout fancy, you'll get major points for serving this clever concoction on Taco Tuesday. My daughter, Ella, asks for this recipe at least once a week. When I initially started making these, I used large shrimp, which can be hard to manage inside a taco shell; it turned out rock shrimp are the perfect size, though they are not always readily available. If you can't find rock shrimp at your local seafood market, you can use large shrimp and cut them into smaller pieces before seasoning. Head to the frozen section in your grocery store and buy the size you like best. The tacos pair very well with the Best Skinny Margaritas (page 202). Serves 4.

For the taco spice seasoning:

- 2 teaspoons chili powder

- 2 teaspoons ground cumin

- 1 teaspoon salt

- ½ teaspoon onion powder

- ½ teaspoon garlic powder

- ½ teaspoon smoked paprika

- ¼ teaspoon cayenne pepper

For the cilantro lime dressing:

- ½ cup sour cream

- ¼ cup olive oil

- Zest and juice of 1 lime

- 2 teaspoons agave syrup

- ½ cup chopped scallions

- ½ cup chopped fresh cilantro

- 1 garlic clove

- ½ teaspoon salt

For the tacos:

- 1½ pounds raw rock shrimp

- 1 tablespoon olive oil

- 1 cup cooked black beans

- 1 (8.75-ounce) can fire-roasted corn

- 2 ounces Mexican Cotija cheese, plus more for garnish

- 2 cups shredded green cabbage

- 8 taco shells or soft tortillas

To make the taco spice seasoning:

In a small bowl, whisk together the chili powder, cumin, salt, onion powder, garlic powder, and cayenne pepper. Set aside.

To make the cilantro lime dressing:

In a blender or food processor, combine the sour cream, olive oil, lime zest and juice, 2 tablespoons of water, the agave syrup, scallions, cilantro, garlic, and salt and purée until smooth. Set aside.

To make the tacos:

In a medium bowl, mix together the shrimp and the taco spice mixture until evenly coated. In a medium skillet, heat the olive oil over medium-high heat. Add the shrimp and sauté, stirring often, until the shrimp are cooked through, 5 to 8 minutes. Set aside.

In a small saucepan over medium-low heat, combine the black beans, corn, and Cotija cheese and cook, stirring occasionally, until warm, about 5 minutes.

In a medium bowl, combine the cabbage and about ¾ cup of the cilantro lime dressing and set aside.

To assemble the tacos:

Fill the tortillas with the shrimp; black beans, corn, and cheese mixture; and dressed cabbage, in that order. Serve with the remaining cilantro lime dressing and additional Cotija cheese on the side.

SNAPPER PICCATA

—

The savory taste of this lemon, butter, and white wine sauce with capers over fish has made it a melt-in-your-mouth favorite in our family. The secret addition of cornstarch to the flour really helps the light coating stay on the fish while it cooks. Where we live in South Florida there is a wide variety of snapper available, such as red, hog, mutton, and yellowtail. All are delicious, and if you don't have access to those varieties, another mild, white, flaky fish will work nicely. Serves 4.

- ¾ cup all-purpose flour

- ½ cup cornstarch

- ½ teaspoon salt

- ½ teaspoon black pepper

- 1½ pounds snapper fillets, skinned and bones removed

- 5 tablespoons butter, divided

- 1 tablespoon olive oil

- 2 garlic cloves, minced

- ½ cup white wine

- Juice of 1 lemon plus 1 lemon, sliced

- ¼ cup capers, drained

- Chopped fresh parsley, for garnish

In a shallow dish, whisk together the flour, cornstarch, salt, and pepper until combined. Dredge the fish in the flour mixture, making sure to coat both sides. Set aside on a plate.

Continued

In a 15-inch nonstick skillet over medium-high heat, heat 3 tablespoons of the butter and the olive oil until slightly bubbly. Add the fish and cook until golden brown, 5 to 6 minutes on each side. Depending on the size of the fish fillets, you may need to cook the fish in batches (add an extra 1 tablespoon of butter and ½ tablespoon of oil to the next batch if that's the case). Transfer the fish to a serving plate and cover with aluminum foil to keep warm.

Add the remaining 2 tablespoons of butter and the garlic to the skillet and cook until the garlic starts to brown, 3 to 4 minutes. Add the wine, lemon juice, and capers, remove from the heat, and stir until combined. Pour the sauce over the fish. Garnish with parsley and lemon slices and serve immediately.

GROUPER WITH MACADAMIA AND GRAPES

—

This dish was inspired by our travels to Iceland. We rented a camper with our kids and explored the majestic west fjords, searching for nothing in particular and happening upon everything spectacular. And then we found Tjoruhusid, a fish restaurant in an old Danish whaling community that served whatever was fresh out of the ocean that day. Located in the town of Isafjordur in a former cod-drying house that was built in 1781, the restaurant seats guests at long wooden communal tables, dimly lit with votives. It was a Modern Hippie's dream come true! The restaurant served a recipe very much like this one and it knocked our boots off. I came home, stood in my kitchen, and tried to re-create it. The original dish was made with cod, which is plentiful in Icelandic waters, so I used grouper, which is popular around the Florida coast. Any white, mild-tasting (preferably locally caught) fish that is available to you will suffice. It's not exactly the same as Chef Maggi's dish, but it comes awfully close. Serves 4.

- 1 cup macadamia nuts

- 3 to 4 tablespoons butter, divided

- 1½ pounds grouper fillets or other white, mild-tasting fish, bones removed

- 1 large shallot, chopped

- 1 garlic clove, minced

- 1 cup chopped white mushrooms

- ¾ cup halved seedless red grapes

In a small skillet over medium-high heat, toast the macadamia nuts until fragrant and darker brown in color, 3 to 5 minutes. Transfer to a small bowl and set aside.

In a 15-inch nonstick skillet over medium heat, melt 2 tablespoons of the butter until slightly bubbly. Add the fish and cook until golden brown, about 5 minutes on each side. Depending on the size of the fish fillets, you may need to cook the fish in batches (add an extra tablespoon of butter to the next batch if that's the case). Transfer the fish to a serving plate and cover with aluminum foil to keep warm.

Add the remaining 1 tablespoon of butter, the shallot, and garlic to the skillet and cook until the shallot is translucent and fragrant, 3 to 5 minutes. Add the mushrooms and grapes and cook, stirring often, until the mushrooms are soft, 3 to 5 minutes. Pour the ingredients from the pan over the fish and serve immediately.

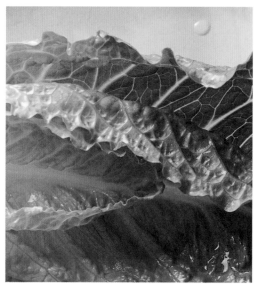

TERIYAKI CHICKEN LETTUCE WRAPS

—

Everyone loves these wraps when I serve them as an appetizer, but why not serve them for dinner? It's easy to make the chicken mixture ahead of time and it's satisfyingly healthy. I serve it with lettuce leaves, but another delicious way to serve it is over a bed of chopped iceberg lettuce. I strongly suggest doubling this recipe for leftovers because it's just as good the next day. Serves 4.

- ¼ cup hoisin sauce

- 1 tablespoon tamari or soy sauce

- 1 tablespoon rice vinegar

- 2 teaspoons Sriracha sauce (optional)

- 1½ teaspoons sesame oil

- 1 teaspoon honey

- 4 teaspoons olive oil, divided

- 1 pound ground chicken

- ⅔ cup sliced scallions

- ½ cup shredded carrots

- 2 garlic cloves, minced

- 1½ teaspoons grated ginger

- 1 (8-ounce) can water chestnuts, drained and diced

- 1 large head Bibb or iceberg lettuce, leaves rinsed and separated

In a medium bowl, whisk together the hoisin sauce, tamari, rice vinegar, Sriracha, sesame oil, and honey. Set aside.

In a nonstick skillet over medium-high heat, heat 2 teaspoons of the olive oil. Add the ground chicken and, using a spoon, break up the meat into small pieces. Cook until no longer pink in the middle, about 5 minutes. Drain the excess liquid and transfer the chicken to a plate.

Add the remaining 2 teaspoons of olive oil to the skillet, add the scallions and carrots, and sauté until soft and fragrant, about 2 minutes. Add the garlic and ginger and sauté for 2 minutes more. Add the chicken back to the skillet with the vegetables and add the water chestnuts. Pour in the hoisin sauce mixture and mix well until everything is evenly coated. Serve warm or chilled in lettuce cups.

PESTO CHICKEN MARGARITA

—

For those looking for another go-to chicken recipe, your family will appreciate this easy weeknight meal that packs in the flavor and looks impressively gourmet. The unique tomato and pesto topping over lightly broiled mozzarella cheese is a simple yet elevated way to serve this modern comfort chicken dish. Serves 4.

- 4 boneless skinless chicken breasts
- 4 tablespoons olive oil, divided
- 1 teaspoon garlic powder
- 1 teaspoon Italian seasoning
- ¼ teaspoon salt
- ¼ teaspoon black pepper

- 1 cup cherry tomatoes, quartered
- ¼ cup thinly sliced fresh basil
- 1 tablespoon fresh lemon juice
- 4 thick slices mozzarella cheese
- ½ cup basil pesto

Preheat the oven to 350°F.

Place 1 chicken breast in a large plastic storage bag and pound it with a mallet or hammer until it's approximately ½ inch thick. Repeat with the rest of the chicken. In a large bowl, combine the pounded chicken breasts, 2 tablespoons of the olive oil, the garlic powder, Italian seasoning, salt, and pepper. Toss until evenly coated.

In a separate medium bowl, mix together the tomatoes, basil, and lemon juice.

In a large oven-safe skillet over medium-high heat, heat the remaining 2 tablespoons of olive oil. Add the chicken breasts and cook until browned, about 5 minutes per side. Transfer the skillet to the oven and bake until cooked through, about 15 minutes.

Place 1 slice of mozzarella cheese on top of each piece of chicken. Turn the oven to a low broil and broil until the cheese starts to brown and is slightly bubbly, 3 to 5 minutes.

Transfer the chicken to plates, then top each breast with about 3 tablespoons of the pesto and about ⅓ cup of the tomato mixture. Serve immediately.

THE BEST BAKED "FRIED" CHICKEN

—

Who doesn't love fried chicken? And what's better than a healthier baked chicken that tastes exactly like the "real" thing? All you need is five ingredients, a brown paper lunch bag or quart-size plastic bag, and perhaps some buttermilk biscuits! You can thank me later. Serves 4.

- 2 tablespoons Crisco shortening

- 1½ cups all-purpose flour

- 2 teaspoons salt

- 2 teaspoons black pepper

- 4 bone-in skin-on chicken breasts

Preheat the oven to 400°F.

Place the shortening on a large baking sheet and place in the oven for 1 to 2 minutes, or until melted.

Combine the flour, salt, and pepper in the paper or plastic bag and shake gently to mix. Place 1 chicken breast at a time inside the bag, fold the top of the bag to seal, and shake until the chicken is evenly coated. Place the chicken on the baking sheet, skin-side down. Repeat with the remaining breasts.

Bake for 30 minutes. Using tongs, flip over the chicken and bake for an additional 40 minutes. Let cool for 10 minutes before serving.

WHOLE ROASTED LEMON HERB CHICKEN

—

My family loves this juicy rotisserie-style chicken recipe, and I love how easy it is to pull off on a weeknight. I like to serve it with the sides I suggested in the menu on page 115 and with (canned!) cranberry sauce for that feel-good, home-cooked weeknight feast. When the savory aromas of fresh cut herbs start wafting around the house, my kids always walk in the door and say, "Wow, the house smells so good! What's cooking?" Serves 4.

- 1 (4- to 5-pound) whole roasting chicken

- 3 lemons, 1 juiced and 2 sliced

- 2 tablespoons olive oil

- 3 garlic cloves, minced

- 1 tablespoon chopped fresh rosemary

- 1½ teaspoons salt

- 1 teaspoon chopped fresh sage

- 1 teaspoon chopped fresh thyme

- ½ teaspoon black pepper

- 1 cup dry white wine

Preheat the oven to 425°F. Place an oven rack in the lowest position. Place a rack in a small roasting pan.

Place the chicken on the rack and pat the skin dry with paper towels. Remove the giblets from the chicken cavity and insert the slices from 1 lemon and the halves from the juiced lemon.

Continued

In a small bowl, combine the olive oil, lemon juice, garlic, rosemary, salt, sage, thyme, and pepper. Rub the mixture evenly over the skin of the chicken, covering the legs and wings and even rubbing underneath the skin where possible. Pour the white wine into the roasting pan. Arrange the remaining lemon slices in the pan with the wine.

Roast the chicken for about 1½ hours, basting the chicken with the pan juices every 30 minutes, until the juices run clear when you cut into it. Remove from the oven and cover the chicken with aluminum foil until just before you are ready to carve and serve. Arrange the carved chicken on a serving platter and pour the juices from the pan over the top of the chicken. Serve immediately.

Easy Weeknight Feast Menu

WHOLE ROASTED LEMON HERB CHICKEN (page 113)

SWEET POTATO CASSEROLE (page 160)

STEAMED GREEN BEANS

—

SET THE SCENE

Prepare the potatoes earlier in the day or even the day before and refrigerate. Steam the green beans while the chicken is roasting.

Assign a member of the family to create a playlist for dinner. Background music enhances the meal and encourages kids and teenagers to actively participate in the planning of the evening.

Make it easy and set one small bunch of flowers in a low vase in the center of your table.

Use place mats and cloth napkins. Cloth napkins don't always make a table more formal, but they do show an element of intention that your family will notice.

CHRISTIAN'S CLASSIC ITALIAN PASTA

—

We are pasta lovers at heart. A couple of decades ago, Christian and I spent our honeymoon in Italy, and on that trip we fell in love with Italian food and wine. A simple and flavorful tomato sauce won us over, so we bought a cookbook about classic Italian cooking. Christian enjoys the art of cooking as much as he loves feeling like he's back in Italy. So he spent years perfecting this dish, which became a family favorite and we think it's cookbook-worthy. It's evolved to become *his* special recipe. To this day, his version of a true Italian red sauce remains one of his best creations yet, and I can just picture the dish towel hanging over this shoulder. Whether we are at home or renting a vacation home on our travels, this is a dish we go to when we want a good comfort meal. Serves 4 or 5.

- 2 tablespoons olive oil

- 1 medium white onion, chopped

- 3 large garlic cloves, minced

- ½ teaspoon black pepper

- 3 (½-inch-thick) slices pancetta, diced

- 8 ounces white mushrooms, sliced

- 1 (28-ounce) can whole peeled tomatoes

- 1 (8-ounce) can tomato sauce

- ½ cup (1 stick) butter

- ¼ cup Italian red wine (or whatever red you're drinking with dinner)

- ½ teaspoon salt

- ½ cup grated Parmesan, plus more for garnish

- ¼ cup chopped fresh basil, plus more for garnish

- 1 pound rigatoni pasta

In a 12-inch skillet with 3-inch sides, warm the olive oil over medium-high heat. Add the onion, garlic, and black pepper and cook until the garlic starts to brown, about 4 minutes. Add the pancetta and cook, stirring often, until fragrant and crispy, about 5 minutes. Add the mushrooms and cook, stirring often, for another

3 minutes. Pour the peeled tomatoes and the tomato sauce into the skillet and, using a spatula, break up the tomatoes into smaller pieces. Add the butter, wine, and salt, turn the heat down to medium, and cook, stirring occasionally, until the sauce is thick and bubbly, 30 to 45 minutes.

Just before serving, turn the heat to low and stir in the Parmesan and basil.

While the sauce is cooking, bring a 4-quart pot of salted water to a boil. Add the rigatoni and cook until al dente, 11 to 12 minutes. Reserve 1 cup of the pasta water and set aside. Drain the pasta and add it directly to the skillet with the sauce and toss until evenly coated. Add some of the reserved pasta water in small increments and stir until combined, until it reaches your desired consistency. Garnish with the extra basil and grated Parmesan cheese. Serve immediately.

FIVE-INGREDIENT TAGLIATELLE WITH PROSCIUTTO

—

Tagliatelle is a thin fettuccine and is one of my favorite types of pasta to use for simple sauces. I just love a delicious pasta recipe that's perfect for a weeknight dinner yet impressive enough to serve to guests. Impressive and simple channels your inner Modern Hippie. I came up with this combination of flavors by adding delicately sweet yet salty prosciutto to one of my favorite classic Italian pasta dishes, cacio e pepe. You'll be surprised at how flavorful these five ingredients can be when they come together, plus you can whip it up at the last minute, serve it with a bottle of Italian table wine such as Chianti, and wow your guests. *Bellissima!* Serves 4.

- 1 pound tagliatelle pasta

- 6 tablespoons unsalted butter

- 2 (8-ounce) packages sliced prosciutto, chopped into bite-size pieces

- 1 cup grated Pecorino Romano cheese, plus more for garnish

- 1½ teaspoons black pepper

Bring an 8-quart pot of salted water to a boil. Add the tagliatelle and cook until al dente, 8 to 10 minutes. Reserve ½ cup of the pasta water, drain the pasta, and set aside.

While the pasta is cooking, melt the butter in a 12-inch skillet over medium-high heat until golden and bubbly, about 3 minutes. Add the prosciutto and cook until crisp, 5 to 7 minutes. Remove the pan from the heat.

Return the pasta to the empty pot and add the prosciutto. Add the Pecorino, pepper, and reserved pasta water and mix until combined. Spoon the pasta into individual bowls and top with extra grated cheese.

TEN-MINUTE SMOKY TOMATO PENNE

—

For a quick meatless red sauce with a twist, try this. The cream cheese and smoked paprika (one of my favorite spices) give the sauce a bit of a smoky and creamy à la vodka taste. This is my go-to meal on weeknights when my kids have sports and we don't feel like getting takeout. Not only can you make this in ten minutes, but it's also an economical meal to double or triple for a large family gathering. Serves 4.

- 1 pound penne pasta

- 1½ tablespoons olive oil

- 1 medium yellow onion, chopped

- 2 garlic cloves, minced

- 1 (15-ounce) can diced tomatoes

- ½ teaspoon dried oregano

- ½ teaspoon dried basil

- ½ teaspoon salt

- 2 tablespoons tomato paste

- ¼ cup cream cheese, softened

- ¼ cup grated Parmesan cheese, plus more for garnish

- ½ teaspoon smoked paprika

Bring a 4-quart pot of salted water to a boil over high heat. Add the pasta and cook until al dente, about 10 minutes. Reserve ½ cup of the pasta water, drain the pasta, and set aside.

In an 8-quart pot, heat the oil over medium heat. Add the onions and garlic and sauté until the onions are soft and fragrant, 3 to 5 minutes. Add the diced tomatoes and their juices, oregano, basil, and salt and stir until combined. Turn the heat to low, add the tomato paste, cream cheese, and reserved pasta water, and cook, stirring constantly, until the cream cheese is melted, about 1 minute. Add the Parmesan cheese and smoked paprika and cook, stirring constantly, until the cheese has melted, about 2 minutes. Add the cooked pasta and stir until evenly coated.

Spoon the pasta into individual bowls, top with extra cheese, and serve immediately.

HOMEMADE PIZZA TWO WAYS

—

When I have company over for dinner and I want a sophisticated yet fun atmosphere with good conversation, I throw a homemade pizza party! In our family, we try to eat gluten-free as much as possible. With plenty of premade gluten-free pizza crust options that taste really great in the frozen section of grocery stores, I'll buy several, as well as a variety of prepared and fresh ingredients for sauce and topping variations. Before anyone arrives, I create the pizza with the sauces and toppings of my choice and have them ready to pop in the oven after cocktails. To serve, I like to place a large piece of butcher or parchment paper directly on the kitchen counter or table and place the pizzas on top. For a slightly different presentation, I cut the pizza into smaller squares instead of slices, so that it functions like finger food, yet it's hearty enough to count as dinner. I encourage you to try the Smoked Salmon Pizza, which was inspired by a meal we had in Rome one New Year's Eve at a little cafe on the cobblestone streets of the Jewish Ghetto. Each pizza serves 2 or 3.

Pesto Caprese Pizza

- 1 (12-inch) regular or gluten-free premade pizza crust
- ⅓ cup store-bought pesto
- 3 thick slices fresh mozzarella cheese
- 1 large tomato, sliced
- ½ cup shredded mozzarella cheese

Preheat the oven to 425°F. Place a large sheet of aluminum foil on the bottom of the oven to catch any melted cheese that may fall off the pizza.

Place the pizza crust on a sheet of parchment paper. Spread the pesto on the pizza crust, leaving a ¾-inch border. Arrange the mozzarella and tomato slices in a single layer, overlapping if necessary. Sprinkle on the shredded mozzarella cheese.

Continued

Slide the pizza off the parchment paper directly onto the middle rack of the oven and bake for about 15 minutes, or until the cheese is melted and bubbly and the crust is golden. Transfer the pizza to a cutting board and let cool for 5 minutes. Cut the pizza into squares or small slices and serve immediately.

Smoked Salmon Pizza

- 1 (12-inch) regular or gluten-free premade pizza crust
- 2 tablespoons olive oil
- 1 large tomato, sliced
- 1 cup grated mozzarella cheese
- 4 ounces cold-smoked sockeye salmon, broken into 1-inch pieces
- 1 cup packed baby arugula
- ⅓ cup shaved Parmesan cheese
- Store-bought balsamic glaze

Preheat the oven to 425°F. Place a sheet of aluminum foil on the bottom of the oven to catch any melted cheese that may fall off the pizza.

Place the pizza crust on a sheet of parchment paper. Rub the olive oil evenly over the pizza crust. Arrange the tomato slices on the pizza. Sprinkle with the mozzarella, leaving about a ¾-inch border.

Slide the pizza off the parchment paper directly onto the middle rack of the oven and bake for about 15 minutes, or until the cheese is melted and bubbly and the crust is golden. Transfer the pizza to a cutting board and let cool for 5 minutes.

Arrange the smoked salmon on the pizza and scatter the arugula and Parmesan on top. Drizzle with balsamic glaze. Cut into squares or small slices and serve immediately.

 Tip: If you're making more than three pizzas, assemble them in advance, place each one on a parchment-lined, rimmed baking sheet, and stack them. This is ideal if you have limited countertop space and the baking sheets will allow enough space so that the sauce is not squished. Bake two or three at a time on different racks in the oven. Cut the baked pizzas into squares or slices and arrange them on butcher paper for your guests. Pop the next batch in the oven while everyone is eating the first batch. I don't recommend making homemade pizzas for any more than twelve to fifteen people, because you'll spend all your time baking pizza instead of having fun.

MOM'S MEATLOAF

—

Warning! This is delicious, hearty, and the ultimate cozy comfort food. This traditional meatloaf has been passed down for three generations, and each time I make it, I can see my mom and grandmother's hands when I look down at my own hands and mix the ingredients together. I serve it just like they did, with mashed potatoes and green beans. This serves quite a few people, so I usually make it for a large extended family dinner, or I make it for the four of us and deliver leftovers to my neighbors and friends. This is a great meal to make the day before and refrigerate. It also freezes well for up to 3 months when wrapped in plastic wrap and stored in a freezer-safe container. To reheat, let it sit at room temperature (or defrost if from the freezer) for 45 minutes before baking. Serves 8 to 10.

For the sauce:

- 1 (28-ounce) can crushed tomatoes

- 1 (14.5-ounce) can petite diced tomatoes

- 1 (15-ounce) can tomato sauce

- 1 tablespoon garlic salt

- 1 tablespoon onion powder

- 1 tablespoon granulated sugar

For the meatloaf:

- 3 pounds ground chuck

- 1 pound ground pork

- 1 pound mild or hot breakfast sausage

- 1¼ cups diced white onion

- 1 cup lightly crushed salted crackers, such as Ritz

- ½ cup Italian bread crumbs

- ¼ cup ketchup

- 3 tablespoons Worcestershire sauce

- 1 tablespoon yellow mustard

- 1 tablespoon black pepper

- 1 tablespoon garlic salt

- 1 tablespoon onion powder

To make the sauce:

In a medium bowl, combine the sauce ingredients and stir well. Set aside.

To make the meatloaf:

Preheat the oven to 350°F.

In an 11-by-15-inch glass baking dish, working with your hands (gloves can be used), mix together the ground chuck, ground pork, breakfast sausage, onion, crackers, bread crumbs, ketchup, Worcestershire sauce, mustard, black pepper, garlic salt, and onion powder, making sure to combine well. Form the mixture into the shape of a loaf that is rounded on the top (alternatively, you can divide the meat in half to make two smaller loaves in separate pans). Bake for 45 minutes.

Remove the meatloaf from the oven and, using paper towels, carefully soak up the grease from the sides of the meatloaf. (Caution: The grease will be very hot.) Pour the sauce over the meatloaf so that it evenly covers the entire loaf. Bake for another 30 minutes, or until the sauce is bubbling. Remove from the oven and spoon more of the sauce from the baking dish over the top of the loaf.

Let cool for 5 minutes, then slice and serve with extra sauce spooned on top of each piece.

 Tip: Cold ground meat can make for cold hands. Remove the meat 30 minutes before you start mixing the ingredients together.

POT ROAST WITH CARROTS AND ONIONS

—

Each year during the holidays, Grammy would serve a version of this savory and comforting pot roast. The aromas of this meal throughout your house is enough to become ingrained in your senses. This recipe was not written down, but I did my best to re-create it from memory and I've been carrying on the holiday tradition in my own home in recent years. I also make this on nights where we will be having two or three extra guests for company because it's a great meal to make ahead and heat in the oven just before serving. I love the way the sweet and sour flavors in the tomato sauce taste with the tender, melt-in-your-mouth beef. The carrots and onions make this a complete meal in itself, so once you put it in the oven, you can relax and look forward to sharing it with your family. This is a meal you'll want to start earlier in the day, as it takes several hours in the oven for that fall-apart tenderness. Serves 5 to 7.

- 1 (3- to 4-pound) brisket or bottom round roast
- Garlic salt
- Black pepper
- 2 tablespoons olive oil, divided
- 1 large white onion, sliced lengthwise
- 5 garlic cloves, finely chopped

- 1 (1-pound) bag baby carrots
- 1 (28-ounce) can crushed tomatoes
- 1½ cups beef broth
- ¼ cup apple cider vinegar
- ¼ cup brown sugar
- 1 tablespoon tomato paste

Preheat the oven to 350°F.

Season the brisket with garlic salt and black pepper on all sides. In a large skillet over medium-high heat, heat 1 tablespoon of the olive oil. Add the brisket and cook on all sides until golden brown, 2 to 3 minutes per side. Transfer the brisket to a plate and set aside.

In the same skillet, heat the remaining 1 tablespoon of olive oil over medium-high heat. Add the onions and garlic and sauté until soft and golden brown, 3 to 5 minutes. Place the brisket in the center of a large roasting pan and scatter the onions and garlic evenly around the sides. Scatter the carrots around the brisket.

In a medium bowl, mix together the crushed tomatoes, beef broth, apple cider vinegar, brown sugar, and tomato paste. Pour the mixture evenly around the veggies, spooning some of the sauce over the top of the brisket. Cover the pan tightly with foil, making sure to tent it at the top so it doesn't touch the brisket.

Roast for 5 hours, or until the brisket is tender and falls apart when pulled with a fork. Turn off the oven and keep the brisket in the warm oven until ready to serve. Place the roast on a serving platter with the carrots and onions and the extra sauce. To serve, pull the meat apart with two forks.

GIRLS CAN GRILL!

Okay, gentlemen, move over.
Girls can grill too, and boy do we love
to turn up the heat!

When you're grilling food, a hot fire alone is not the only element you need to know about. Using an oil to cook with that has a high smoke point is key. Smoke point is a measure of an oil's tendency to generate smoke when it reaches certain high temperatures and every oil has a different smoke point. Because a grill gets really hot, you'll want an oil with a higher smoke point so it can withstand those higher temperatures. Some oils with high smoke points suitable for grilling are avocado, canola, corn, grapeseed, peanut, and sunflower. The grill is not the place for your extra-virgin olive oil. Burned oil will ruin the taste and texture of your meat.

Before you grill, you'll want to oil the grates of your grill with one of the oils listed above to prevent your food from sticking. You can do this by dipping a wadded paper towel in oil—just enough to coat but not saturate the paper towel. Before the grill is turned on and while the grates are still cool, wipe the oil evenly over the grates. Then, turn on your grill and let the oil burn until it starts smoking, or 15 to 20 minutes before you start cooking. When you grill red meat or poultry, sear the outside first with the flames, which locks in the juices and heat. You can accomplish this by having the grill on high heat, keeping the grill cover open to supply oxygen to the fire, and making sure that you use a high–smoke point oil in the marinade or rubbed directly onto the meat before cooking. Once your meat has that crispy texture on the outside, turn down the heat to medium and cover the grill. Closing the grill takes some oxygen away from the fire, which creates convection like an oven, making the heat more evenly distributed in order to cook the interior of the meat to your desired temperature. Knowing where the hot spots are on your grill will teach you how to move the meat around to either speed up or slow down the cooking process. Grilling food requires your attention. Do not walk away for a long period of time. You should have control over your fire at all times.

Once your meat is done cooking, transfer it to a platter or cutting board and let it rest for 5 minutes. It's important to know that meat continues to cook while it sits, so factor that into your cooking time. Once all the food is off the grill, turn the heat to high to carbonize any food fragments left on the grate, about 15 minutes. Then, using a grill brush, scrape off all the food remnants.

Now that you know the grilling basics, here are three of my favorite recipes to impress.

TENDER, CRISPY BARBECUE RIBS

—

One of my mom's secret recipes are these juicy-on-the-inside, crispy-on-the-outside ribs. Many people throw raw ribs on the grill and they usually end up burning them in order to make sure the inside is fully cooked, but they never get tender that way. Our secret is that you slowly cook the ribs in the oven for hours first. Finish them off on the grill and they'll have a juicy, fall-off-the-bone texture on the inside and a crispy barbecue sauce–flavored texture on the outside. Serves 4 to 6.

- 2 tablespoons garlic salt

- 2 tablespoons onion powder

- 2 tablespoons black pepper

- 2 large racks baby back ribs

- 1 (18-ounce) bottle sweet barbecue sauce of your choice

- 1 (18-ounce) bottle spicy or smoky barbecue sauce of your choice

- Avocado or canola oil

Preheat the oven to 350°F.

In a small bowl, combine the garlic salt, onion powder, and black pepper and whisk until combined. Set aside.

Cover the bottom of a large baking sheet with foil and place the ribs on the sheet. Season both sides of the ribs with the seasoning mixture. With the meaty side of the ribs facing up, cover the pan with aluminum foil, running your fingers along the edge to make sure the foil is sealed tightly to allow the ribs to steam. Bake for 2 hours.

Continued

In a medium bowl, mix together both bottles of the barbecue sauce and set aside.

Remove the ribs from the oven, and carefully remove the top layer of foil, watching out for the steam as it escapes. Oil the grates of your grill to prevent your food from sticking. Turn the grill to medium-high. Paint one side of the ribs generously with the barbecue sauce mixture. Transfer the ribs to the hot grill with the sauce-side down. The ribs are already cooked through, so you'll only need to sear them until they are crispy, 3 to 5 minutes.

While the ribs are searing on the grill, carefully paint the other side of the ribs with the sauce, flip them over, and sear for another 3 to 5 minutes. Paint with sauce again and repeat on each side two or three times, decreasing the amount of time they cook on each side by 1 minute, which will build a thicker and crispier layer of sauce. Remove the ribs from the grill, transfer them to a cutting board, and let cool for 5 minutes.

Using a sharp knife with a long narrow blade, cut the ribs apart. Transfer them to a serving platter and serve with the extra barbecue sauce on the side.

THE JUICIEST BURGERS

—

Oh, I think I make a pretty mean burger. My secret is mixing bun pieces into the beef, which locks in the juices while the burgers are cooking and makes these the juiciest burgers you'll ever eat. This recipe is all about the meat, so make sure you purchase the best you can find. If you have some leftover homemade Montreal steak seasoning from the "Pittsburgh Style" New York Strip Steak (page 140), it is a delicious alternative to the everything bagel seasoning. You might even be impressed with yourself when you make these burgers, so go ahead and pat yourself on the back! Serves 4 or 5.

- 1½ pounds ground chuck

- 1 small yellow onion, chopped

- 2 tablespoons everything bagel seasoning

- 1 tablespoon black pepper

- 6 brioche hamburger buns

- Avocado or canola oil

- 4 or 5 slices American cheese (optional)

In a large bowl, using very clean hands or gloves, mix together the ground beef and onion. Add the everything bagel seasoning and black pepper and mix until combined. Pull apart one of the burger buns into ½-inch pieces and work them into the meat mixture. Divide the meat mixture into 4 or 5 equal portions, and form them into thick patties.

Oil the grates of your grill to prevent your food from sticking to the grates. Turn the grill to high. Carefully place the burgers on the grill. Since ground chuck is high in fat, the burgers will trigger a larger flame. With the grill cover open, sear the burgers for 3 to 4 minutes on each side. Remove the burgers from the grill if you like them on the rare side. Or turn the grill to medium heat or close the cover and continue cooking until they reach your desired doneness, 3 to 5 minutes. This is the time to add cheese if you are doing so. Turn off the grill, transfer the burgers to the buns, place on a platter, and serve immediately.

Grill It, Girl Menu

THE JUICIEST BURGERS (page 137)

TOSSED GREEN SALAD WITH HONEY MUSTARD DRESSING (page 91)

GRILLED CORN ON THE COB WITH PARMESAN
AND PARSLEY (page 151)

—

SET THE SCENE

In the morning, prep the burgers and shuck the corn to save on time later. Make the salad dressing ahead of time and store in the fridge.

Instead of using flowers as centerpieces, wow guests with a "condiments centerpiece" creation. I like to use a medium shallow crate lined with parchment or newspaper to display all the condiments and toppings. Spoon the condiments into small shallow mason jars or ramekins instead of placing bottles of ketchup and mustard on the table. Stack tomatoes, onions, and grilled slices of pineapple in between the small jars.

Using foliage and flowers from around your yard if possible, fill in the holes between the condiments and toppings for a beautiful garnish.

"PITTSBURGH STYLE" NEW YORK STRIP STEAK

—

If you can nail a perfectly cooked juicy steak that's crispy on the outside and rare or medium-rare on the inside, you've got skills and you have achieved the "Pittsburgh style" technique. This is a popular way to enjoy steak and you can use it no matter how you like it cooked on the inside. I like buying a thick cut of organic beef and seasoning it with a traditional mixture of spices. It may take some practice to cook steak to your desired doneness, but don't give up. Remember that once you take your meat off the grill, it will continue to cook while you let it sit before serving. So be sure to take it off just before it's actually done. I usually use the spice mixture below, which is easy to make and can be doubled or tripled so you have it on hand. If you are pressed for time, the Montreal-style steak seasoning blend from the grocery store is a good alternative. You can store the homemade spice mix in a sealed mason jar in the pantry for up to 6 months. Serves 4.

- 1 tablespoon coarse salt

- 1 tablespoon coarse ground black pepper

- 1 tablespoon paprika

- 1½ teaspoons dried minced garlic

- 1½ teaspoons dried minced onion

- 1½ teaspoons red pepper flakes

- 4 New York strip steaks

- 2 tablespoons avocado or canola oil, plus more for coating the grill grates

In a small bowl, whisk together the salt, black pepper, paprika, garlic, onion, and red pepper flakes.

Remove the steak from the refrigerator 30 minutes prior to cooking.

Oil the grates of your grill to prevent your food from sticking. Turn the grill to high. Rub the oil evenly over both sides of the steaks. Season each side with roughly I teaspoon of the steak seasoning mixture. When the temperature of the grill reaches 400°F, place the steaks on the grill and let the flames come above the grates to sear the steaks. Using long grilling tongs, carefully move the steaks back and forth on the grill to add friction, which fuels the fire. Grill for about 4 minutes with the grill cover open. Flip the steaks and sear for about 4 minutes more.

When the steaks are crispy on both sides, turn down the heat to medium and cook the steaks to your desired temperature, 3 to 5 minutes. Turn off the grill, transfer the steaks to a wooden cutting board, and let rest for 5 to 10 minutes. Slice against the grain and serve.

ON THE SIDE

POPOVERS WITH HONEY DRIZZLE

—

Oh, my heart! These towering, golden baked beauties taste as good as they look and warm my soul with a touch of my childhood. My mom would make these for special occasions as an alternative to a traditional dinner roll. I make these in a popover pan, which has taller cups than a standard muffin pan. They will allow the popovers to have a more defined "mushroom" top with a pillowy texture when pulled apart. It is fine to use a muffin pan, it will just make smaller popovers and yield about two more for a total of eight popovers. These make great conversation starters because they are puffy and unique in appearance and so heavenly to eat! They remind me of a mix between a biscuit and a croissant. And with honey drizzled on top—well, it doesn't get much better than that! I love to serve these with the Best Baked "Fried" Chicken (page 111). Makes 6 popovers.

- 1¼ cups all-purpose flour

- 1 teaspoon salt

- 1¼ cups whole milk, slightly warmed

- 3 large eggs, at room temperature

- 1 tablespoon unsalted butter, melted, plus 2 tablespoons unsalted butter, cut into 6 equal pieces

- Cooking oil spray

- Honey, for drizzling (see Tip, next page)

Preheat the oven to 425°F. Place the popover pan in the oven.

In a large bowl, mix together the flour, salt, milk, eggs, and melted butter.

Continued

Place one piece of butter into each cup, and return the pan to the oven until the butter is bubbly, 1 to 2 minutes. Remove the pan from the oven and spray the tops and insides of the cups with cooking oil spray.

Fill each cup two-thirds full with the batter and bake for 20 minutes. Turn the temperature down to 300°F and continue baking for another 5 to 8 minutes, or until the popovers are golden brown on top.

Remove the pan from the oven and, using tongs, carefully transfer each popover from the pan to a cooling rack. Let them cool for 5 minutes. Transfer the popovers to a platter or a napkin-lined basket and serve with honey on the side for drizzling.

Tip: As an alternative to honey, jam and butter are nice accompaniments to popovers.

Simply Southern Menu

WHISKEY ON THE ROCKS (page 193)

WATERMELON, FETA, AND MINT SKEWERS (page 58)

THE BEST BAKED "FRIED" CHICKEN (page 111)

TOSSED GREEN SALAD WITH HONEY MUSTARD DRESSING (page 91)

POPOVERS WITH HONEY DRIZZLE (page 145)

—

SET THE SCENE

In the South, hospitality is simple—good food and good comfort come first—so you'll want to set the scene with that in mind. Choose classic white or ivory plates and clear textured glasses. Set a tall glass carafe or pitcher of water in the middle of the table. Layer a couple of different neutral-colored cloth napkins for place mats, slightly staggering them so that each layer is visible. Fold another one into a rectangle, using the same color as the bottom layer of the place mat to use as a napkin. Using the same fabric in different ways at each setting with neutral complementary colors will juxtapose nicely with the rich and colorful food array, creating a casual but elegant Southern tablescape.

Make the chicken first and, while it is cooking, make the popover batter. When the chicken is done, set it aside while the popovers are baking. Put the chicken back in the hot oven while the popovers cool.

Playing a soft background mix of music will encourage conversation to be in the forefront. Create a playlist of your favorite country songs or queue up a premade list from the Internet.

BROCCOLINI WITH ORANGE ZEST

—

Orange zest is one of my favorite ingredients to use in my cooking and baking, and in this recipe it perfectly complements the broccolini, a cousin of broccoli with smaller florets and more tender stems. It adds a pop of fresh citrus flavor and a touch of sweetness and makes an ordinary vegetable extraordinary. Try serving these with the Snapper Piccata (page 103). Serves 4.

- 2 bunches broccolini

- 2 tablespoons olive oil

- I teaspoon grated orange zest

- ½ teaspoon salt

- ½ teaspoon black pepper

Preheat the oven to 375°F.

Trim about 2 inches off the ends of the broccolini stems and cut any thick stalks in half lengthwise. Place the broccolini on a baking sheet, drizzle with the olive oil, sprinkle with the orange zest, salt, and black pepper, and toss until evenly coated. Spread out the broccolini into a single layer.

Roast for about 15 minutes, or until the broccolini is crisp and tender. Serve immediately.

ROASTED TARRAGON CARROTS

—

I started pairing fresh carrots with tarragon after watching the movie *Ratatouille* with my kids when they were young. This movie really encouraged me to experiment with spices I'd never used before, and opened my eyes to the idea that just one spice can turn vegetables into a side dish loaded with flavor. And speaking of flavor, in this recipe I use ghee instead of butter because I think the flavor is richer, and it's a healthier alternative for those who are sensitive to lactose and casein. These carrots pair well with the Whole Roasted Lemon Herb Chicken (page 113). Serves 4.

- 1 pound carrots, sliced ½ inch thick
- 1 tablespoon ghee or butter
- 1 teaspoon dried tarragon
- ¼ teaspoon salt
- ¼ teaspoon black pepper
- ⅛ teaspoon onion powder

In a steamer pan, fill the water just below the steamer basket and bring to a boil over high heat. Alternatively, use a metal strainer or colander to act as a steamer basket and choose a saucepan that's wide and deep enough to hold the strainer. Turn down the heat to medium, add the carrots, cover with a lid, and steam until tender, 10 to 12 minutes. Carefully remove the steamer basket and pour out the water. Transfer the carrots to the pan and turn the heat to low. Add the ghee, tarragon, salt, pepper, and onion powder and stir until combined. Serve immediately.

GRILLED CORN ON THE COB WITH PARMESAN AND PARSLEY

—

Say goodbye to plain ol' corn. The crisp taste of grilled corn on the cob rolled in Parmesan cheese, smoked paprika (my favorite spice!), and fresh parsley will be your new favorite side to accompany whatever you have cooking on your grill, such as the Juiciest Burgers (page 137). I love to embellish the flavor of corn with cheeses, herbs, spices, and enhanced butters, which is butter with the addition of some sort of spice or chopped vegetable, such as charred scallions, chopping them finely and mixing them with butter. The combinations are nearly endless. Serves 4.

- 4 ears corn on the cob, husks and silks removed
- 2 tablespoons avocado oil or canola oil
- Salt and black pepper

- ½ cup grated Parmesan cheese
- ¼ cup finely chopped fresh parsley
- ½ teaspoon smoked paprika

Turn a gas grill to high heat.

Drizzle the corn with the oil, turning to make sure they're evenly coated. Sprinkle with your desired amount of salt and pepper. Place the corn on the cooler part of the grill so that the indirect heat allows it to cook slowly, close the lid, and cook for 5 minutes. Using tongs, turn the corn over and continue to grill for another 5 minutes, or until the corn is slightly darker in color. Transfer the corn to the main grill rack and let it cook on the hot grates, turning often, for an additional 3 to 4 minutes, or until you just start to see grill marks on the corn. Transfer the corn to a small platter.

In a shallow, rimmed dish, mix together the Parmesan cheese, parsley, and smoked paprika. Roll one ear of corn at a time in the mixture until well coated. Serve immediately.

GINGER RICE WITH TOASTED COCONUT

—

White rice is a staple for many families, but eating it plain can be a little unexciting. So, in this recipe, I've jazzed up everyday white rice using ghee or butter and this sweet duo of ginger and coconut, which adds a ton of flavor with very little effort. Toasting the coconut adds a slightly crunchy texture, while the ghee adds a rich, nutty butteriness that is really delicious. I also like to make white rice with toasted garlic and scallions for another slightly different taste sensation. I make this rice as a side to fish dishes like the Snapper Piccata (page 103). Serves 4 or 5.

- 2 cups white rice

- 1 tablespoon ghee or butter

- ½ cup shredded sweetened coconut flakes

- 1 teaspoon grated ginger

- ½ teaspoon salt

Cook the rice according to the package directions and add the ghee just before covering the pan.

In a small saucepan, heat the coconut flakes over medium heat, stirring often, until brown and toasted, about 4 minutes. Add the coconut flakes, ginger, and salt to the rice and stir until well combined. Serve immediately.

Spice Flight Menu

SNAPPER PICCATA (page 103)

GINGER RICE WITH TOASTED COCONUT (page 152)

ROASTED TARRAGON CARROTS (page 149)

—

SET THE SCENE

Make the carrots and rice first and keep them warm on the stove, so that you can focus your attention on the fish.

Set the scene with a boho-rustic elegance, which will look beautiful when serving fish as the main course. Instead of using a tablecloth, use a fabric runner, place mats, and a charger to frame the plate.

Use greenery or other beautiful pieces from nature that are available to you, such as acorns, leaves, or twigs, to adorn the center of the table. Light a few small candles in votives in between.

Use neutral-colored cloth napkins tied with natural jute twine or use wooden napkin rings. Slide in small twigs with a single dried flower or fresh herbs into the napkin rings for a nice finishing touch.

CHEESY BAKED ZUCCHINI

—

Mom, this one has you all over it! Zucchini can taste a bit bland by itself, but just like with white rice, adding some cheese and spices is an easy and delicious way to spruce up the flavor. Mom used to serve this with Tender, Crispy Barbecue Ribs (page 133). My whole family loves this dish and I love it even more because I can assemble it ahead of time and put it in the oven just in time to be served. Serves 4 to 6.

- 3 large or 4 medium zucchini, cut into ½-inch slices

- 2 tablespoons butter

- ¼ cup grated Parmesan cheese

- ½ teaspoon salt

- ½ teaspoon black pepper

Preheat the oven to 350°F.

In a 9-by-13-inch broiler-safe baking dish, arrange the zucchini slices in a domino fashion, layering one piece slightly over the other. Cut the butter into about 8 small cubes and place each cube in a different spot on top of the zucchini. Sprinkle with the Parmesan cheese, salt, and pepper.

Bake for 20 minutes. Turn the oven to broil and cook until the cheese is golden brown, 2 to 3 minutes. Let cool for 5 minutes before serving.

BALSAMIC BRUSSELS SPROUTS

—

I avoided Brussels sprouts when I began cooking for my family because they were a vegetable I didn't care for—or so I thought. It wasn't until I started tasting creative versions of them in restaurants that I discovered they can be not only delicious, but something I actually crave! Cooked until crispy and finished with a drizzle of sweet balsamic glaze, these are the epitome of modern comfort. Brussels pair well with red meat, such as "Pittsburgh Style" New York Strip Steak (page 140). To save time, you can buy pre-shaved Brussels sprouts from the grocery store. Serves 4.

- 1 pound Brussels sprouts

- 2 tablespoons olive oil

- ¼ teaspoon sea salt

- ¼ teaspoon black pepper

- 1 tablespoon store-bought balsamic glaze

Preheat the oven to 425°F.

On a cutting board, trim the ends off the sprouts. Using a small sharp knife, cut the sprouts in half or into quarters if they're big.

On a baking sheet, combine the sprouts, olive oil, salt, and pepper and toss until evenly coated.

Bake for 20 to 30 minutes, or until the sprouts are crispy and lightly charred on the outside. Remove from the oven and drizzle the balsamic glaze over the sprouts. Serve immediately.

ROASTED RED CABBAGE WITH GORGONZOLA AND HAZELNUTS

—

If you're tired of making the same five veggie sides from memory, consider red cabbage, which I think is one of the most underrated vegetables. When it is roasted and then topped with creamy Gorgonzola cheese and sweet smoky hazelnuts, you'll wonder why it took you so long to try this purple garden goddess. And a drizzle of honey over the top doesn't hurt either. Try serving this with Tender, Crispy Barbecue Ribs (page 133). Serves 4 to 6.

— ⅓ cup chopped hazelnuts

— I head red cabbage, cut into 4 to 6 (¾-inch-thick) rounds

— I tablespoon olive oil

— Coarse salt and black pepper

— ⅓ cup crumbled Gorgonzola cheese

— Honey, for drizzling

Preheat the oven to 400°F. Line a baking sheet with parchment paper.

In a small skillet over medium heat, toast the hazelnuts, tossing frequently, until golden and fragrant, about 4 minutes. Set aside.

Place each slice of cabbage on the prepared baking sheet in a single layer. Using a basting brush, brush the olive oil evenly over the cabbage and season with salt and pepper.

Roast for 40 to 45 minutes, or until the cabbage is tender and the edges are golden. Transfer to a serving platter, sprinkle the Gorgonzola cheese and hazelnuts over the top of the slices, and drizzle with honey. Serve immediately.

LOADED TWICE-BAKED POTATOES

—

Who doesn't love a baked potato loaded with sour cream, bacon, and cheese? It's a meal in itself, and I like to serve these with a basic side salad or as a side dish with the "Pittsburgh Style" New York Strip Steak (page 140). Serves 4.

- 4 large russet potatoes

- ½ cup sour cream

- 2 tablespoons butter, melted

- 6 slices cooked bacon, chopped into large bits

- ½ cup chopped scallions

- Salt and black pepper

- 1 cup shredded Cheddar cheese

Preheat the oven to 400°F.

Using a fork, poke holes in the potatoes in several places to allow for even heat distribution while it bakes. Place the potatoes in a baking dish, cover with foil, and bake for 1½ hours, or until the potatoes are soft when poked with a fork. Let the potatoes cool just until you can pick them up with your hands. Cut the top one-third lengthwise off the potato and set aside. Using a spoon, scoop out the insides of the potato tops and bottoms, making sure to leave about ¼ inch around the inside of the bottom potato sections, and place in a medium bowl. Set the skins aside.

Turn the oven to a low broil.

Mash the potatoes in the bowl. Add the sour cream, butter, bacon, scallions, and salt and pepper to taste and stir until well combined. Stuff the potato skins with enough filling so that it makes a dome on the top. Evenly distribute the cheese on top. Place the potatoes on a baking sheet. Broil until the cheese is melted, about 2 minutes. Let cool for 5 minutes before serving.

SWEET POTATO CASSEROLE

—

Sweet potatoes are my daughter's favorite vegetable, so I love coming up with different ways to serve them. This side dish brings Thanksgiving to mind each time I make it, and it reminds me of a version my mom makes each year, though you can certainly make this recipe at any time of year. Pumpkin pie spice and toasted pecans make this taste more like a dessert than a vegetable! For a Southern-style family meal, pair this recipe with the Whole Roasted Lemon Herb Chicken (page 113). Serves 6.

- 2 cups pecans

- 3 large sweet potatoes, peeled and cut into 1- to 2-inch cubes

- ½ cup oat milk

- 3 tablespoons pure maple syrup

- 3 tablespoons butter

- 2 teaspoons salt

- 1 teaspoon pumpkin pie spice

- ½ teaspoon ground cinnamon

- 1 cup dark brown sugar

In a small skillet over medium heat, toast the pecans until fragrant and dark brown, 3 to 5 minutes. Set aside.

Place the sweet potato cubes in an 8-quart pot and fill with enough water to cover the potatoes by 1 to 2 inches. Bring to a boil over high heat and cook until the potatoes are soft when poked with a fork, about 30 minutes. Drain the potatoes and transfer them to a large bowl. Using a potato masher, mash the potatoes until fluffy. Add the oat milk, maple syrup, butter, salt, pumpkin pie spice, and cinnamon and stir until well combined.

Preheat the oven to 425°F.

Spread the potatoes evenly into a 9-by-13-inch baking dish. Top evenly with the brown sugar and pecans and bake until the brown sugar is bubbling, about 10 minutes. Serve immediately.

ROSEMARY ONION MAC AND CHEESE

—

I haven't met many people who didn't grow up eating boxed macaroni and cheese. Well, my fellow mac 'n' cheese lovers, this is the "adult" version (though it's rated G for all audiences to consume). Savory, sweet, and a tad smoky, it is my favorite dish of indulgence because it tastes like Christmas. Serve it with the Winter Berry Salad (page 83) to complete the comforting holiday feel for your table on any day of the year. Oven-safe skillets are great for transferring dishes from your stove top to the oven, and this recipe is a perfect candidate for that cooking method, giving you golden topping perfection. I buy a prebaked piece of cornbread or corn muffins from my grocery store to save time. I recommend making this dish ahead of time and finishing it off in the oven just before you're ready to serve. Serves 8.

- 12 ounces large elbow macaroni pasta

- 1 cup crumbled cornbread

- 1 cup shredded Gruyère cheese, divided

- 2 tablespoons unsalted butter, melted, plus 5 tablespoons unsalted butter, divided

- 3 teaspoons salt, divided

- 1½ teaspoons chopped fresh rosemary, divided

- 2 garlic cloves, minced

- 1 large red onion, thinly sliced

- 1 tablespoon apple cider vinegar

- 1 tablespoon honey

- 3 tablespoons all-purpose flour

- 2½ cups milk or plant-based milk

- 3 cups shredded Cheddar cheese

- 1½ cups shredded Parmesan cheese

- 1 teaspoon dry mustard

- 1 teaspoon black pepper

- ¼ teaspoon smoked paprika

Continued

Preheat the oven to 425°F.

Bring a 4-quart pot of salted water to a boil over high heat. Add the pasta and cook, stirring occasionally, until al dente, 6 to 8 minutes. Drain and rinse. Set aside.

In a small bowl, combine the cornbread crumbles, ½ cup of the Gruyère, the 2 tablespoons of melted butter, ½ teaspoon of the salt, and 1 teaspoon of the rosemary.

In a 12-inch cast-iron skillet, heat 2 tablespoons of butter over medium-high heat. Add the garlic and cook until fragrant, about 2 minutes. Add the onion and cook, stirring occasionally, until soft, 6 to 8 minutes.

Add the vinegar, honey, and remaining ½ teaspoon of rosemary and cook, stirring, until the liquid is absorbed, about 2 minutes. Transfer the onion mixture to a bowl and set aside. Carefully wipe the skillet clean with a paper towel.

Melt the remaining 3 tablespoons of butter in the skillet over medium heat. Add the flour and cook, stirring constantly with a whisk, until golden and bubbly, about 2 minutes. Increase the heat to medium-high. Gradually add the milk, whisking frequently until thickened, about 5 minutes. Remove the skillet from the heat and gradually stir in the Cheddar, Parmesan, and remaining ½ cup of Gruyère. Stir in the dry mustard, pepper, smoked paprika, and remaining 2½ teaspoons of salt. The sauce will be thick. Add the cooked pasta and onion mixture and stir until well mixed. Smooth into an even layer in the skillet. Top with the cornbread mixture.

Bake for about 10 minutes, or until the topping is golden brown. Serve immediately.

DESSERTS

CINNAMON BUN TWISTS

—

If I had to pick my last meal, these cinnamon bun twists would be on the menu. Each chewy twist is baked to perfection and has the perfect amount of cinnamon and icing, plus there's no messy cutting involved, which makes these the ultimate finger food dessert. For as long as I can remember, my Aunt Patti was the baker on my dad's side of the family, and we made never-ending requests for her famous "giraffe swirls," which is what we used to call them when we were kids. Each soft, chewy twist is like a three-bite cinnamon bun and will leave you wanting to double the recipe next time. Serves 4 to 6.

- ⅓ cup brown sugar

- 4 tablespoons butter, melted, divided

- 2 tablespoons ground cinnamon

- 1 (8-ounce) can refrigerated crescent rolls, such as Pillsbury

- 1 cup confectioner's sugar

Preheat the oven to 375°F. Line a baking sheet with parchment paper.

In a small bowl, mix together the brown sugar, 3 tablespoons of the melted butter, and cinnamon and set aside.

Remove the crescent rolls from the can and unroll them onto a cutting board. Using the perforations as a guide, separate the dough into four rectangles, pressing the unused perforations together to seal the dough. Spread two of the rectangles with the butter mixture. Place the other two rectangles on top to form two sandwiches. Using a sharp knife, cut each dough sandwich into four small rectangles. Twist each small rectangle twice and place on the prepared baking sheet, making sure to press the ends onto the baking sheet.

Bake for 10 to 15 minutes, or until golden brown. Let cool on a cooling rack for 5 minutes.

While the rolls are baking, in a small bowl, mix together the confectioner's sugar, remaining 1 tablespoon of melted butter, and 1 teaspoon of hot water until smooth. Drizzle the icing evenly on top of the warm twists and serve immediately.

NEW YORK–STYLE CRUMB CAKE

—

I grew up on Entenmann's crumb cake, and as a kid, I didn't think there was anything better. Now I'm a grown-up and I've created my own homemade version of a super-moist sour cream cake with cinnamon sugar crumbles on top. Actually, it has extra cinnamon crumbles, because in my opinion, there were never enough for my liking, and because the crumbs that fell on the plate were the best part! It's possible that Grammy loves this cake more than she loves me. I like to make a whole cake for her, cut it into squares, and wrap each square in foil. She loves to take one piece from the freezer each morning, reheat it, and enjoy it for breakfast with her coffee. Serves 12 to 14 or one Grammy.

For the crumb topping:

- 1¼ cups dark brown sugar

- ½ cup granulated sugar

- 1½ tablespoons ground cinnamon

- 1 teaspoon salt

- 1 cup unsalted butter, melted

- 3 cups all-purpose flour

For the cake:

- 2½ cups all-purpose flour

- 1 teaspoon baking soda

- ½ teaspoon baking powder

- ½ teaspoon salt

- ¾ cup unsalted butter, at room temperature

- 1 cup granulated sugar

- 3 large eggs, at room temperature

- 1 cup sour cream, at room temperature

- 2 teaspoons vanilla extract

- Confectioner's sugar, for dusting

Continued

Preheat the oven to 350°F. Grease a 9-by-13-inch baking dish.

To make the crumb topping:

In a medium bowl, mix together the brown sugar, granulated sugar, cinnamon, and salt. Add the melted butter and flour and mix gently with a fork. Do not overmix; there should be large crumbles.

To make the cake:

In a large mixing bowl, whisk together the flour, baking soda, baking powder, and salt. Set aside.

In a small bowl, mix together the butter and granulated sugar until smooth and creamy. Add the eggs, sour cream, and vanilla and mix until combined. Pour the wet mixture into the dry mixture and stir until smooth and thick.

Spread the batter evenly into the prepared baking dish and top with the crumb topping, pressing lightly down into the cake.

Bake for 45 minutes, or until a toothpick inserted into the center comes out clean. Let cool completely on a cooling rack, 30 to 40 minutes.

Using a sifter, dust the confectioner's sugar over the top. Cut into 2-inch squares. Serve at room temperature. The cake can be stored in an airtight container for up to 4 days.

New York at Home Menu

YOUR FAVORITE MARTINIS

MANDARIN ORANGE AND RED ONION SALAD (page 84)

"PITTSBURGH STYLE" NEW YORK STRIP STEAK (page 140)

LOADED TWICE-BAKED POTATOES (page 159)

NEW YORK-STYLE CRUMB CAKE (page 169)

SET THE SCENE

Make the crumb cake in the morning (and have some for breakfast!).

Premake the salad and reserve the dressing until ready to serve. The loaded baked potatoes can be premade and refrigerated until ready to bake.

Go for a chic tablescape with a warm, yet eccentric, vibe. Vibrantly colored glassware can make everyday meals look more fun. Set the table with mismatched textured water goblets. Use white or neutral-colored plates to highlight the glassware.

Arrange a few clear glass votive candles around the table mixed with glass hurricanes with pillar candles inside. Dim the overhead lights so that the low candle lighting reflects the colors of the fun glassware.

EASY BUNDT CAKE

—

I have a secret to tell you. I do not use an electric mixer—ever. I find them bulky and heavy and very difficult to clean. So when I bake, I always mix by hand. If you can relate, then this cake is calling your name. It's the cake that will make you look like the baker you've always wanted to be. Introduced to me by my mom's best friend, Tricia, this moist and delicious cake is as easy as it gets. In fact, it's so effortless that when your guests keep coming back for "just one more small piece," you'll almost feel guilty. And that's because the truth is this cake is a combination of boxed cake mix and instant pudding mix. The result is a tender cake with a smooth and silky chocolate icing that melts in your mouth. It's the perfect cake to throw together when you need a guaranteed crowd-pleaser, but you don't have time to make something else. Shhh. I won't tell. Serves 8 to 10.

For the cake:

- 1 (15.25-ounce) box vanilla cake mix (see Tip, next page)

- 1 (3.4-ounce) package vanilla instant pudding mix (see Tip, next page)

- 4 eggs

- 1¼ cups water

- ½ cup vegetable oil

For the icing:

- 1 (14-ounce) can sweetened condensed milk

- 1 cup semisweet chocolate chips

- 1 teaspoon vanilla extract

- Rainbow sprinkles (optional)

To make the cake:

Preheat the oven to 300°F. Generously grease the inside of a Bundt pan.

In a large bowl, mix together the cake mix, instant pudding mix, eggs, water, and vegetable oil until smooth and combined. Pour the batter into the prepared Bundt pan.

Continued

Bake for 55 minutes, or until a toothpick inserted into the cake comes out clean. Let cool on a cooling rack until completely cool, about 1 hour. Transfer the cake to a cake plate or platter.

To make the icing:

In a small saucepan over medium heat, combine the condensed milk and chocolate chips and stir constantly until the chips are melted and the consistency is smooth, 3 to 5 minutes. Remove from the heat and stir in the vanilla. Let the mixture cool for about 10 minutes. Store the cake on a covered cake platter or another airtight container for up to 4 days.

Spread the icing over the cake using a small spatula, allowing the icing to drip around all sides. Top with sprinkles if desired, slice, and enjoy. Store the cake on a covered cake platter or another airtight container for up to 4 days.

 Tip: Try other flavors of cake mix—whatever is your favorite. I often make this with chocolate cake mix and chocolate instant pudding mix. It's fun to experiment!

CRISPY RICE OATMEAL CHOCOLATE CHIP COOKIES

—

Crispy rice in chocolate chip cookies? Yes, please! Each time I make these, I think of my Aunt Jan, who introduced them to the family years ago. Today, I love to make a big batch of these and store them on a covered cake plate in my kitchen. It warms my heart when my kids' friends come over and lift up the glass cover to take one before heading out to the skate ramp in the backyard. Whenever I eat them, I feel like a kid again. Makes 2 to 3 dozen cookies.

- 1 cup butter, at room temperature
- 1 cup brown sugar
- 1 cup granulated sugar
- 2 eggs
- 1 teaspoon vanilla extract
- 2 cups all-purpose flour
- 1 teaspoon baking soda
- 1 teaspoon baking powder
- ½ teaspoon salt
- 1 cup rolled oats
- 1 cup crispy rice cereal
- 1 (12-ounce) bag chocolate chips

Preheat the oven to 350°F. Line a baking sheet with parchment paper.

In a large bowl, mix together the butter, brown sugar, and granulated sugar until well creamed. Add the eggs and vanilla and continue mixing until smooth.

In a small bowl, whisk together the flour, baking soda, baking powder, and salt. Add the dry ingredients to the creamed mixture and mix until combined. Add the rolled oats, crispy rice cereal, and chocolate chips and stir until well combined. Cover the bowl with plastic wrap and refrigerate for 30 minutes.

Spoon the cookie dough onto the prepared baking sheet in 1½-inch balls. Bake for 12 to 15 minutes, or until golden brown. Let cool on a cooling rack for 5 minutes before serving. These cookies will keep well in an airtight container at room temperature for up to 5 days.

LAVENDER ROSE BUTTER COOKIES

—

While baking cookies for a holiday cookie exchange, I noticed my botanical cooking herbs on the counter from making the Fancy Bohemian cocktail (page 197). I remembered I had purchased a bottle of lavender cooking extract from a farmers' market in New York City and I wanted to experiment with it, so I began playing with different ingredients to make these enchanting, buttery beauties. Look online for lavender extract, dried lavender, and rose petals for cooking. Makes 2 to 3 dozen cookies.

- 1 cup unsalted butter, at room temperature

- ¾ cup granulated sugar, plus more for sprinkling

- 1 egg, at room temperature

- ½ teaspoon almond extract

- ½ teaspoon lavender extract

- 2 cups all-purpose flour

- ¼ cup almond flour

- ½ teaspoon salt

- 1½ tablespoons dried edible rose petals, plus more for garnish

- 2 teaspoons dried lavender, plus more for garnish

Preheat the oven to 350°F.

In a large bowl, mix together the butter and granulated sugar until well combined. Add the egg, almond extract, and lavender extract and mix until combined. Slowly add the all-purpose flour, almond flour, and salt and continue to mix until combined. Gently fold in the dried rose petals and lavender until well distributed.

Using a piping bag with a decorative tip, pipe the dough into 2-inch circles on an ungreased baking sheet. Sprinkle each of the cookies with a pinch of sugar and a few buds of lavender and/or rose petals.

Bake for 12 to 15 minutes, or until the cookies are golden brown on the edges. Transfer the cookies to a wire rack to cool before serving. These cookies will keep well in an airtight container at room temperature for up to 5 days.

GLUTEN-FREE PEANUT BUTTER CHOCOLATE CHIP COOKIES

—

There is so much to love about these cookies. First, you'd never guess that they have no flour in them. Second, you need only five ingredients. Third, they take less than 15 minutes to make from start to finish. But the best part is that they are loaded with soft and chewy deliciousness! That's why these are my daughter Ella's favorite thing to bake. Makes about 2 dozen cookies.

- 1 cup creamy peanut butter

- 1 egg

- 1 cup chocolate chips

- 1 cup brown sugar

- 1 tablespoon baking soda

Preheat the oven to 350°F. Line a baking sheet with parchment paper.

In a large bowl, mix together the peanut butter, egg, chocolate chips, brown sugar, and baking soda until well combined. Spoon the cookie dough onto the prepared baking sheet in 1-tablespoon portions. Bake for 12 to 15 minutes, or until the cookies are golden brown and firm on top. Repeat with any remaining dough, using fresh parchment paper for the second batch. These cookies will keep well in an airtight container at room temperature for up to 5 days.

CHOCOLATE ALMOND BUTTER BANANA BITES

—

When I have extra bananas lying around that I want to enjoy before they get overly ripe, I like to cover them in chocolate! This is my husband's favorite dessert and it's the perfect guilt-free sweet treat. I keep them in the freezer and he grabs one when he is in need of a little indulgence. Makes 25 to 30 bites.

- 3 ripe bananas
- ½ cup natural almond butter
- 1 teaspoon coconut oil
- 1 cup semisweet chocolate chips
- Coarse sea salt

Line a baking sheet with parchment paper.

Peel the bananas and slice ¼ inch thick. Place half the banana slices on the prepared baking sheet and spread about ½ teaspoon of almond butter onto each slice. Top with the remaining banana slices to form little sandwiches. Place the baking sheet in the freezer until the bananas are frozen, about 1 hour.

In a medium saucepan over medium-low heat, melt the coconut oil until it shimmers, about 3 minutes. Add the chocolate chips and melt, stirring often to keep the chocolate from burning. Turn the heat to the lowest setting to keep the mixture warm.

Remove the baking sheet from the freezer and dip each banana sandwich into the chocolate, coating only halfway. Remove any excess chocolate off the bottom of the banana by scraping it on the side of the saucepan. Return the bites to the baking sheet and sprinkle a small pinch of sea salt over each one. Return the baking sheet to the freezer until the chocolate is set, about 45 minutes.

Transfer the bites to a freezer-safe container and store for up to 3 weeks.

VEGAN CHOCOLATE DONUTS WITH STRAWBERRY ICING

—

All of your indulgent donut dreams will come true when you bite into these insanely delicious guilt-free donuts. (Yes! I said guilt-free!) I created these a few years ago when we had friends for dinner who were vegan. I wanted them to have something elegant, delicious, and a little fun, and these vegan donuts proved to be just the right choice. They were a big hit then, and to this day I continue to experiment with vegan donut flavors in my kitchen. The rose petals are the ultimate sprinkle on top. For vegans and non-vegans alike, these donuts taste even better than the "real" thing. Makes 6 donuts.

For the donuts:

- 1 cup all-purpose flour

- ½ cup almond flour

- ½ cup unsweetened cocoa powder

- 2 teaspoons baking powder

- ½ teaspoon baking soda

- ¼ teaspoon salt

- ¾ cup full-fat oat milk or plant-based milk

- ¼ cup unsweetened applesauce

- 3 tablespoons avocado oil

- ¼ cup brown sugar

- ⅛ teaspoon almond extract

- ¼ cup agave syrup

For the icing:

- 2 cups confectioner's sugar

- 1 tablespoon strawberry jam

- 2 tablespoons plant-based milk

- 1 tablespoon warm water

- Edible rose petals, crumbled (see Tip, next page)

Continued

Preheat the oven to 375°F. Grease a 6-cavity donut pan.

To make the donuts:

In a medium bowl, whisk together the all-purpose flour, almond flour, cocoa powder, baking powder, baking soda, and salt until well combined.

Add the oat milk, applesauce, avocado oil, brown sugar, agave, and almond extract and stir until combined. Spoon the mixture equally into each cavity in the donut pan, wiping away any excess with a paper towel.

Bake for 10 minutes, or until the donuts are puffy and bounce back when touched. Let cool on a cooling rack for 5 minutes. Remove the donuts from the pan, making sure the rounded "pretty" sides are facing up. Let the donuts cool completely.

To make the icing:

Place a sheet of parchment paper underneath a cooling rack to catch the icing drippings.

In a medium bowl, mix together the confectioner's sugar, strawberry jam, plant-based milk, and water until well combined and thick. Dip the rounded side of each donut into the icing, submerging just enough to coat the top of the donut. Place each donut back on the wire rack. Repeat the icing dip for each donut, which will ensure thickly glazed donuts. Sprinkle a pinch of the edible rose petals on top. Serve immediately or place the donuts in an airtight container in the fridge for up to 24 hours.

 Tip: Edible rose petals can be purchased online. Alternatively, you can pick the dried rose petals out of rose tea bags.

CITRUS HERB FRUIT SALAD

—

By now you probably know my love affair with fresh herbs in leafy green salads, so it's only fitting that they make an appearance in one of my favorite sweet treats. I'm often asked to bring a fruit salad to my mother-in-law's house as a contribution to the dessert array, and I'm pretty sure it's because I know how to pair organic seasonal fruit that's more than the ordinary mixture of melon and pineapple. Sure, anyone can cut up fresh fruit in a bowl and call it a salad, but this recipe is especially delicious because it combines the fruits I love with the refreshing twist of lemon, basil, and mint. I try to buy organic fruits and herbs when possible. If some of the fruits I call for are not in season or available to you, choose another variety of fresh fruit. Serves 6 to 8.

- 1 tablespoon fresh lemon juice
- 1 teaspoon agave syrup
- ⅛ teaspoon sea salt
- 2 peaches, pitted and sliced
- 1 cup strawberries, sliced

- 1 cup red grapes, halved
- ½ cup raspberries
- ½ cup blackberries
- ¼ cup fresh basil leaves, torn
- ¼ cup fresh mint leaves, torn

In a small bowl, whisk together the lemon juice, agave syrup, and sea salt.

In a large serving bowl, toss together the peaches, strawberries, red grapes, raspberries, blackberries, basil, and mint. Drizzle the dressing on top and toss until coated evenly.

DRINKS

A MODERN MANHATTAN

—

When I was in my mid-thirties, I visited the famous Dewberry Hotel bar in Charleston, South Carolina, and I had my first Manhattan cocktail. From that moment on, it was my drink of choice because I loved its smoky flavor and the sweet brandied cherry garnish, which appealed to every one of my senses. Something about this drink transports me to a mid-century Southern living room bar with period furnishings, brass finishes, and classic jazz playing on the turntable. And those brandied cherries aren't just part of the garnish—they're an absolute must in my opinion, and you can find them in most liquor stores. Serves 2.

- 4 ounces bourbon

- 2 ounces sweet vermouth

- 8 dashes Angostura bitters (either aromatic or orange)

- 4 to 6 brandied cherries

In a cocktail shaker with ice, combine the bourbon, vermouth, and bitters and shake well. Strain into two chilled coupe glasses and garnish with 2 or 3 cherries each on a metal or wooden skewer.

A GUIDE TO DRINKING WHISKEY

When I'm not enjoying a cocktail, I like to sip a fine whiskey. Whether you enjoy it on the rocks (with ice) or neat (without ice), whiskey is all about the senses. Our favorite whiskey is Japanese, which is harder to find because the demand outweighs the supply. What makes Japanese whiskey different from others is that it undergoes double distilling before being aged in wooden barrels and is therefore drier and smokier compared to sweeter American bourbons and ryes. Whichever you choose, buy the best you can afford and forget the mixers.

WHISKEY NEAT

—

Like anything fine in life, enjoying whiskey slowly is best. I think fine whiskey is best served neat, with maybe a drop or two of filtered water to open it up and allow the nose to experience the rich aromas. If you're trying whiskey for the first time—or the first proper time anyway—start neat. The best type of glass to use for a neat pour is a tulip glass, which is a small glass with a tapered rim that directs the scent to your nose. I prefer a small, old-fashioned lowball cocktail glass because I like seeing the prism of light that the etching on the glass creates, which is part of engaging all the senses. To serve, pour 1½ to 2 ounces into the glass. Hold the glass up to your nose with a slightly open mouth. Inhale. After you take a sip, breathe in through your nose and exhale a long breath out of your mouth. Pay attention to the way it tastes, smells, and feels and take note of your favorite types.

WHISKEY ON THE ROCKS

—

A classy and proper way to serve whiskey is on the rocks in a wide, low cocktail glass with a single large cube or sphere of ice. One large ice cube is preferred over small cubes because smaller cubes melt more quickly and will water down the whiskey too much before you can finish it. A large cube will allow you to sip your whiskey slowly while it remains cold and minimally diluted, which is the best way to enjoy whiskey. You can find ice cube molds for this purpose at liquor stores or online.

FRESH GRAPEFRUIT PALOMAS

—

My good friend LK has a sense of style to be envied, from her fashion sense to her dinner table and—most importantly—to her cocktail glasses. She uses fresh ingredients and she makes sure her drinks look as good as they taste. Admittedly, making homemade simple syrup and dehydrated citrus doesn't make for the quickest of cocktails, but you can make these elements ahead of time, so serving them to your guests is simpler than you might think. This version of a Paloma will leave a lasting impression on your special company. Serves 2 to 4.

For the dehydrated grapefruit slices:

- 2 to 4 grapefruits, thinly sliced

- Sugar, for sprinkling

For grapefruit simple syrup (makes about 2¼ cups):

- 2 cups fresh grapefruit juice

- 2 cups sugar

- 2 tablespoons grapefruit zest

For the cocktails:

- 2 ounces blanco tequila

- 2 ounces fresh grapefruit juice

- Juice of ½ lime

- Soda water (optional)

- Rosemary sprigs

- 1 lime, cut into thin slices

(Optional) To make the dehydrated grapefruit slices:

Preheat the oven to 200°F. Line a baking sheet with parchment paper.

Place the grapefruit slices on the baking sheet in one layer and sprinkle with sugar. Bake for 2½ hours, rotating the pan about halfway through. Let cool completely.

Continued

The grapefruit slices can be stored in an airtight container in a cool, dry place for up to 6 months.

To make the grapefruit simple syrup:

In a medium saucepan, combine the grapefruit juice, sugar, and grapefruit zest and bring to a boil. Turn down the heat to low and simmer, stirring occasionally, for 5 minutes. Strain the liquid through a fine-mesh strainer, pour the liquid into a jar with a lid, and refrigerate. The syrup can be stored in the fridge for up to 1 week.

To make the cocktails:

In a cocktail shaker filled with ice, combine the tequila, grapefruit juice, lime juice, and 1 ounce of grapefruit simple syrup and shake well. Strain the cocktail into martini glasses to serve "up," or pour it into ice-filled cocktail glasses and top with a splash of soda water, to serve it "on the rocks." Garnish with dehydrated grapefruit slices.

THE FANCY BOHEMIAN

—

By now you know about my love of using botanicals in food, such as baking with rose petals and lavender in the Lavender Rose Butter Cookies (page 177). This cocktail reminds me of the time we were in Sonoma, California, for my best friend Ana's wedding. The lavender was in full bloom and love was in the air. I remember I was enjoying a classic gin martini while I gave the bride a toast. This is a tribute to the hybrid of lavender fields and gin martinis, and all of my senses take me back to Sonoma. I prefer to use Hendrick's gin because the lavender plays perfectly with its subtle botanical notes of juniper and coriander. You can buy dried lavender online or in gourmet markets. Serves 1.

For the lavender infusion:

- 2 tablespoons dried lavender buds

- 1 cup boiling water

For the cocktail:

- 2 ounces gin

- ½ ounce dry vermouth

- 1 teaspoon agave syrup

- 1 lemon twist, for garnish

To make the lavender infusion:

In a glass bowl, combine the lavender buds and boiling water and let steep for 30 minutes. Strain through a sieve over a small bowl, cover, and refrigerate until cold. Discard the lavender buds. Store any unused lavender infusion in an airtight container in the fridge for up to 1 week.

To make the cocktail:

In a cocktail shaker filled with ice, combine the gin, vermouth, agave, and ½ ounce of lavender infusion and shake vigorously for 10 seconds. Strain the liquid into a martini glass. Garnish with a twist of lemon.

GOOMBAY PUNCH

—

My husband's family spent summers in the Bahamas while he was growing up, and this was the adult drink of choice, which was adapted from Bahamian culture. The name was inspired by the annual Goombay Summer Festival, which showcases its food and culture. There are many different versions of this punch in the islands, but this is the one that we have made for the last twenty years or so and we think it's the best spiked fruit punch we've ever had. This is a great cocktail to make in big batches for a Fourth of July party or big summer barbecue, and let guests serve themselves from pitchers. The punch is best made 24 to 48 hours ahead to develop the best flavor, so make sure you have plenty of space in your fridge to store it before the big day. Serves a crowd.

- 1 (1-liter) bottle dark rum

- 1 (750-milliliter) bottle coconut rum

- 1 (750-milliliter) bottle apricot brandy

- 1 (128-ounce) container fresh orange juice

- 2 (64-ounce) bottles pineapple juice

In two large beverage containers or punch bowls, divide the dark rum, coconut rum, apricot brandy, orange juice, and pineapple juice equally and stir. Refrigerate for 24 to 48 hours before serving. Serve over ice.

Meet the Neighbors Menu

GOOMBAY PUNCH (page 198)

SINFULLY SUPREME PIZZA DIP (page 52)

STURDY CORN CHIPS FOR SERVING

THE JUICIEST BURGERS (page 137)

CITRUS HERB FRUIT SALAD (page 185)

—

SET THE SCENE

Create a digital menu that you can text to your guests by using a fun background photograph of your backyard or another tropical image.

Remember to make the punch a day or two before, as it's best made in advance! Make the pizza dip and the burgers earlier in the day so that they are ready to bake and grill. Prepare the fruit salad ahead and reserve mixing in the dressing and herbs until just before serving.

Keep the food and serving theme casual with your guests needing only a (plastic or wooden) fork at most and a paper plate. Use prefolded heavy-duty paper napkins.

Set the scene in your backyard. Set up two tables, one for glasses and the pitchers of punch and the other for the food and serving pieces.

Place a burlap tablecloth or runner over the tables and use some natural elements, such as palm leaves. Place low tropical flower arrangements on each table.

If your scene is at night, hang string lights over the tables and arrange some fun glass votives or hurricane lamps on the serving tables.

Create a playlist of Caribbean music or find one online.

MOJITO MOCKTAIL

—

I can't decide what I love more about this mocktail—the fact that it smells so good or that its sweet and tart flavors come directly from the earth. Either way, this drink is my go-to on nights where I want something sophisticated, refreshing, and nonalcoholic (though feel free to add rum or cachaça for the classic cocktail). Bet this will be your new favorite accompaniment to sparkling water. Serves I.

- 4 fresh mint leaves, plus more for garnish

- ½ lime, cut into 4 wedges

- ¾ cup lime-flavored sparkling water

- I tablespoon agave syrup

In a medium cocktail glass, combine the mint and 3 of the lime wedges. Using a small muddle or a wooden spoon, crush the lime and mint just enough to open up the flavors. Fill the glass almost to the top with ice. Add the sparkling water and agave and gently stir. Garnish with the remaining lime wedge and mint.

THE BEST SKINNY MARGARITAS

—

It's hot most of the year where I live in South Florida, and there is no doubt that this "skinny" margarita is the drink of choice in our home, whether we are inside or poolside. It's refreshingly tart and not overly sweet, just the way we like it. The key to a good skinny margarita is using fresh organic ingredients and natural sweeteners. This cocktail is particularly good on Taco Tuesdays, when I often make Cilantro Lime Rock Shrimp Tacos (page 100). If you are making these for a crowd and want a good store-bought option to mix with the tequila, use Tres Agaves Organic Margarita Mix instead of the lime juice, orange juice, and agave. Serves 2.

— 4 ounces tequila blanco, such as Casamigos

— 2 ounces lime-flavored sparkling water

— ½ cup fresh lime juice

— 2 tablespoons fresh orange juice

— ¼ cup agave syrup

— 1 lime, cut into 4 wedges

In a large cocktail shaker filled with ice, combine the tequila, sparkling water, lime juice, orange juice, and agave syrup. Shake gently just to combine and pour into tumblers. Garnish each cocktail with a lime wedge.

Tip: To make a pitcher of margaritas that serves 6 to 8, in a large pitcher, mix together 16 ounces of tequila, 8 ounces of lime-flavored sparkling water, 2 cups of fresh lime juice, ½ cup of fresh orange juice, and 1 cup of agave syrup. Stir well to combine and serve immediately over ice, or cover and refrigerate for up to 3 days. Garnish each glass with a lime slice.

ACKNOWLEDGMENTS

—

First and foremost, thank you to my husband, Christian, for your unwavering support of this book, every step of the way. Your unconditional love and acknowledgment of my journey has opened up a greater love than I have previously known. Our love language of cultivating togetherness within our home is something our children witness daily.

To my children, Ella and Brayden, you have watched me do hard things, and your love and encouragement has been the fuel that keeps me going. I am most proud of our dining room table and the space you fill amongst it. May you always remember that family bonds and friendships are harvested around eating meals together and showing up for one another.

Mom and Dad, hearing you say the words "I'm proud of you" will echo in my ears for the rest of my life, as there is no greater feeling than when a parent tells you this. Dad, your Toasted Buns with Jam are a childhood memory I will cherish forever, and now we get to share them with the world! Mom, you have taught me how to love through cooking, and each time I cook, I carry you with me.

To my grandmother, "Grammy," my love of hosting was the best gift you have ever given to me, and you showed me by example. I adore you and your mantra for a long, good life: Eat, drink, and shop—and do it all in good health! And to my grandmother, "Nana," you are always in my kitchen in spirit. I know you are smiling down when you see your Eggs Benedict in this book!

Kristy, Frankie, Cindy, and Mike—having you as a team in my home made this project so much more than a job for all of us. We became family, and your warmth and talent helped bring out the best in this book. I'll never forget our dance parties after long days! To Chris and AJ, my talented designers, we have never actually met in person, but our teamwork is a true testament that virtual creative connections can not only be possible, but also beautiful. Thank you for all the encouragement and words of wisdom when I needed it most. And wow! Look what we created together!

To *the* one and only Amy Treadwell, my editor, my sunshine, my lifeline throughout the course of writing this book—your gifts extend beyond your creative talents. Your gentle guidance and support has helped restore my faith in the beauty that comes from the breakdown of writing a book.

To the warrior woman and publisher, Angela Engel, and her wonderful team at the Collective Book Studio, thank you for discovering me, for taking a chance, and for believing in me every step of the way. I am so proud to be on this journey together. I hope this is just the beginning!

To all my friends and family who tested my recipes and loved me even when I had little time to nurture friendships while writing this book, thank you for staying. A big shout out to the loved ones whose recipes adorn some of these pages, as you have all touched my heart beyond the kitchen.

And to YOU, the reader, the witness, the believer—thank you for seeing me.

INDEX

—

ABOUT THE AUTHOR

Lauren Thomas decided to write her lifestyle cookbook, *The Modern Hippie Table*, after her blog inspired women to reinvent their passion for the home, have fun in the kitchen, and feel good in their own skin.

Her personal creative endeavors include cooking, entertaining, travel, and fashion and whether she's experimenting with flavors in the kitchen or setting the scene for a beautiful evening, her ultimate goal is to bring people together at the table with good food and conversation. Lauren's recipes and tablescapes demonstrate how the thoughtful execution of simple recipes and beautiful decorations can turn a casual evening into a lasting memory.

Lauren lives in south Florida with her husband, two children, and their Shar Pei pup, Simon. You can connect with Lauren on her lifestyle media platform on Instagram, @the.modern.hippie.way, or by visiting her website at themodernhippieway.com.